For the journal writers who have shared their stories
in these pages with such openness and generosity.
Thank you.

Contents

Creative
Journal
Writing

Creative Journal Writing

the art and heart of reflection

STEPHANIE DOWRICK

JEREMY P. TARCHER/PENGUIN

a member of Penguin Group (USA) Inc.

New York

JEREMY P. TARCHER/PENGUIN
Published by the Penguin Group
Penguin Group (USA) Inc., 375 Hudson Street, New York, New York 10014,
USA • Penguin Group (Canada), 90 Eglinton Avenue East, Suite 700, Toronto, Ontario
M4P 2Y3, Canada (a division of Pearson Canada Inc.) • Penguin Books Ltd, 80 Strand,
London WC2R 0RL, England • Penguin Ireland, 25 St Stephen's Green, Dublin 2,
Ireland (a division of Penguin Books Ltd) • Penguin Group (Australia),
250 Camberwell Road, Camberwell, Victoria 3124, Australia (a division of Pearson
Australia Group Pty Ltd) • Penguin Books India Pvt Ltd, 11 Community Centre,
Panchsheel Park, New Delhi–110 017, India • Penguin Group (NZ), 67 Apollo
Drive, Rosedale, North Shore 0632, New Zealand (a division of Pearson New Zealand
Ltd) • Penguin Books (South Africa) (Pty) Ltd, 24 Sturdee Avenue, Rosebank,
Johannesburg 2196, South Africa

Penguin Books Ltd, Registered Offices: 80 Strand, London WC2R 0RL, England

Most Tarcher/Penguin books are available at special quantity discounts for bulk purchase
for sales promotions, premiums, fund-raising, and educational needs. Special books or book
excerpts also can be created to fit specific needs. For details, write Penguin Group (USA)
Inc. Special Markets, 375 Hudson Street, New York, NY 10014

Library of Congress Cataloging-in-Publication Data
Dowrick, Stephanie.
Creative journal writing : the art and heart of reflection / Stephanie Dowrick
p.   cm.
ISBN 978-1-58542-686-7
1. Diaries—Authorship.   I. Title.
PN4390.D69   2009   2008039920
808'.06692—dc22

Printed in the United States of America
5   7   9   10   8   6

Book design by Cheryl Collins Design

While the author has made every effort to provide accurate telephone numbers and Internet
addresses at the time of publication, neither the publisher nor the author assumes any responsibility for errors, or for changes that occur after publication. Further, the publisher
does not have any control over and does not assume any responsibility for authors or third-
party websites or their content.

How to use this book

One of the essential ingredients of creative journal writing is freedom: freedom from judgments, freedom to write as you wish and only about what interests you. How you will use this book is, necessarily, entirely up to you. But my humble suggestion is that you first read it through like a conventional book, stopping only if an exercise here or there grabs you by the ankle and pulls you to the ground. *Stop here.* If that doesn't happen, experience the ideas and the many wonderful stories as a whole, and only then go back to work your way through it far more personally, engaging with all the exercises that you want, at the pace you want, and in the way you want.

Pleasure is the other essential ingredient of journal writing. So use this book in the way that will give you most pleasure: reading, writing, pausing, setting aside, returning, all at a pace and in a rhythm entirely of your own making.

Whose plans?

It takes courage to do what you want. Other people have a lot of plans for you.

—Joseph Campbell

Getting started

❧

Writing a journal may change your life

I want to write, but more than that, I want to bring out
all kinds of things that lie buried deep in my heart.

—Anne Frank

On thick white pages in a leather-bound book or scribbled across
the backs of envelopes tossed into a cardboard box, written
faithfully through a lifetime or with years in between entries,
written lyrically or as a bare list, journal writing may well be the
most accommodating of all writing forms. It may also be the most
pleasurable.

The impulse to write is natural for many people. Yet the
demands of more public forms of writing can be inhibiting or
even crushing. In the private spaces of your journal, a genuine
sense of possibility is renewed with every blank page. The internal
judge or critic that so often sits between the writer and the page
can be fired. The possibilities of style, mood, and expression that
journal writing offers are limitless.

Journal writing is a supreme way to record your own life's
journey. It is a way to discover what matters to you and even what
and how you think. It is a gloriously self-directed source of inner
development, yet it also makes the world beyond your own self
more real and more vivid. It can become an interface between you
and the outside world. It can become a companion that supports

but doesn't judge. It can be a place of discovery, of learning, of emotional relief and insight. It can also become a playground, where the everyday rules of writing, reflecting, problem solving, goal setting, production, and planning no longer apply.

Without restrictions or censorship your mind can race—or slow down. It can step outside boxes or turn them sideways. It can make utterly fresh connections or simply pause, allowing you to see what is familiar with new eyes. It can train you to observe with subtlety all kinds of situations. And it can help you to learn something of value even from the unwelcome ones.

Journal writing will train and hone your eye for beauty. It will invite you into the present moment (while also allowing you to roam your past). It will let you reexperience awe and wonder. It will let you intensify and renew your pleasure in events and situations that have gone well. It will support your recovery (and the gaining of wisdom) from the times you wish had never happened.

However small the physical pages on which you are writing, your journal is big enough to encompass all of your selves: your intuitive self, your everyday competent self, your dreamy self, your practical self, your uncertain self, and the self who knows just what is needed. This is a place, too, where you can talk to your soul or spirit and hear your soul talk back to you. You can talk to other people, alive or dead; you can release uncomfortable emotions and find new responses.

It is virtually impossible to write a journal and not discover more about yourself. It is absolutely impossible to write a journal and not put your own stamp on it. Every journal is inevitably original. When it comes to journal writing, there is no formula. There are certainly props and prompts. And I share many here. In journal writing, though, these are intended to be liberating, not constricting.

The freshness that comes from writing in this way very naturally permeates your life. A journal consists of observations, insights, memories, impressions, and feelings. It may also include plans and analysis. It may have layers of secrets and trails of jokes. It is the container for dreams and hopes. Sometimes it is actually marked by tears. It is where failures and successes weave to form a texture that can eventually be seen as the reflection of a complex and rich life. Failures or setbacks may matter a little less as the journal helps you increasingly to see your life as a whole. Successes and satisfactions may be valued a little more.

Journal writing is the key to discovering your own unique inner world. Your journal belongs to you, and your journal reflects you. For many journal writers, it is also a guide, a map, a treasure trove, and a repository of memories.

As I write these lines, I am thinking about the chart that was once on the back of my kitchen door, measuring my children's height as they grew. A journal tracks your growth, too, but with greater subtlety. Sometimes it is hard to see how far you have come until you are startled by something you wrote five years ago or maybe only five months ago.

Journal writer Dieter has this to say about writing his journal: "Writing a journal makes you examine your life. As long as you record mainly the positive, you will have hours of reading in old age. You probably wish you could relive your life. You will be."

This view nicely echoes a statement from the writer D. H. Lawrence: "If only one could have two lives: the first in which to make one's mistakes…and the second in which to profit by them."

And American writer Gail Godwin says, "I write for my future self, as well as my present mood. And sometimes, to set the record straight, I jot down a word or two in old diaries to my former self— to encourage, to scold, to correct, to set things in perspective."

Journal writing is all about process, not goals or outcome.

It is freeing, not constraining.

Journal writing is also where you can *retire* the inner critic or judge.

How you write, what you write, matters only to you.

You are writing to please no one but yourself.

Celebrate!

Marco Polo, May Sarton, Thomas Merton, Anaïs Nin, Andy Warhol, Richard E. Grant, Anne Frank, Samuel Pepys, Winston Churchill, Cleopatra, Louis XVI, Rainer Maria Rilke, Virginia Woolf, and Katherine Mansfield are just some of the countless people who have valued the art and practice of journal writing. Each of them, through years of writing about the large and small matters that make up a life, created something absolutely distinct. What they wanted from journal writing, and what they brought to it, reflected their unique interaction of needs, passions, reflections, and aspirations.

In her novel *Fear of Flying*, Erica Jong's heroine, Isadora Wing, reflects on what journal writing has given her: "As I read the notebook, I began to be drawn into it as into a novel. I almost began to forget that I had written it. And then a curious revelation started to dawn. I stopped blaming myself; it was that simple.... [It was] heartening to see how much I had changed in the past four years."

For me, journal writing is the writing and thinking place where I am least inhibited. It's where my great love for words (inherited from both my schoolteacher parents) can pour out without any sense of judgment about what other people will think of what I am doing or saying. Often, though, it is not the words that I am paying most attention to but the thoughts that I am seeking to express. Here, too, there are far fewer moments of self-consciousness or censorship than in most of the other writing that I do. These days I am writing my books, as I have done for more than twenty years now; I am writing my regular "Inner Life" column in *Good Weekend*; I am writing my Interfaith services and material for the talks and retreats that I regularly give; I am writing countless e-mails; and, intermittently but passionately, I continue to write a journal as I have done—sometimes with long gaps—for most of my life.

Throughout this book I describe and demonstrate what is specific for me about journal writing, but the qualities that come first to mind are intimacy and freedom. In fact, it is not only "free"—especially of censorship—it is also freeing.

There is much that I can say or do in the pages of a journal that would be impossible in other writing contexts. I can create a "still life" in words, for example, entirely for my own pleasure: a snapshot that has greater depth and dimension than a photograph ever could. The frustrated painter in me gets tremendous pleasure from that. I can dwell on my family, on my totally personal concerns, without any fears that I am boring anyone or being too self-focused. I can write lovingly and probably sentimentally about our cats. I can copy out prayers or thoughts that support my spiritual development.

Many journal writers who are also professional writers, as I am, use their journals as the place to develop ideas or reflect on their intellectual work in progress. I can see the value of this and have always loved reading journals that include this—lately, for example, and very intensely, the journals of Thomas Merton and Rainer Maria Rilke; earlier, the journals of Virginia Woolf and Anaïs Nin. (May Sarton is also widely read, but she, too, is very focused on domestic details and the natural world, while also writing about her life as a poet and novelist.)

What I have also learned, however, is that admiring a particular style of journal writing, or the way journal writing can be used, is not enough. Journal writing is naturally instinctive, perhaps the most instinctive form of writing that we have. That's why it can be such a powerful support for our creativity generally, if we allow that. And that's why there is no right or "perfect" way to do it. Very directly it reflects what is unique and irreplaceable about each person's internal world.

My own journal writing suffers, in comparison with my professional writing, in that it almost always comes last. The only exception was when I was going through an especially rough patch some years ago (that lasted for several years) and my need was overwhelming for the depth of inner dialogue that *only* journal writing makes possible.

More generally, when I am under a great deal of (self-inflicted) pressure to produce writing in my other fields, it is my journal writing that gets set aside. (Lavish promises to ourselves are not enough.) Yet when I am not writing anything at all in my journal, I know very well what I am missing.

Journal writing is the place where I can be most playful and frivolous, where my life as a mother gets its due prominence, where my immediate physical environment looms largest, where my professional writing life—which truly dominates and drives my waking hours—fades into relative insignificance. Here is a short example, written the night before I was due to teach one hundred people journal writing. It reflects the work I am doing the next day and to some extent was prompted by it. What dominates though, at least from my perspective, is my interior life and my domestic life.

Stephanie Dowrick: Journal extract

Friday, 22 Nov. My room. 9:30 p.m. Still hot and sticky. Insects on overdrive. Griffyn [one of our cats] trying to eat my pen. Gabe [my son] upstairs playing music as he writes. Nick Cave. Kezia [my daughter] out at training. House feels quiet despite Cave. In the cave. Restful. I used to play music while I write far more often than I do now. It feels like a loss, not a choice. Looking forward to the [journal writing] workshop tomorrow. Seems ages since I taught something so relatively straightforward—a lovely way to connect with a big group. *This is what's possible.* Journal writing can give you THIS. And THIS. Griff finding it unbearable that he can't climb onto this journal that's edging him out of his rightful place on my lap. Geraldine [my sister] stayed Tues and Wed nights. What a treat. Small talks but not small talk in our nighties. 'Do you have time to look for a new sofa with me?' 'Maybe, but I would replace the carpet first.' Who else would tell me? How wonderful to have and to still have my sister. Why is Griffyn so much more engaged with pushing in when I am writing than when I am reading? Is he like a child—thinking this is too much engagement that is not to do with him? Or does the moving pen wake up the hunter in him? He can hear my pen move from rooms away. And hear me stir before I have stirred. K. home. Garage door down. Nick Cave retired.

Your journal-writing "voice" and concerns will be no less distinct. And what you get from your journal writing will mirror that. So, are you ready for this? Are you *choosing*?

Writing a journal—this harmless, portable, practically cost-free, and mild-mannered "interest"—can really be life-changing. It can be the companion you need *whatever life is bringing you*. It can also be addictive, surprising, moving, illuminating, and tremendously enjoyable. It can deliver a vast array of invaluable new insights. It lets you "read" your own life even while you are writing it. It lets you see the world around yourself more richly and deeply. The familiar can become newly strange; the strange can become familiar.

It supports you to value your own history, judgments, values, and opinions. (After all, no one knows you better than you know yourself. But sometimes you need to *discover* what you know.) It can give you an invaluable sense of being at the center of your life rather than at the periphery. At the same time, and even when you remain at the center of your own writing, it may make you less anxiously "self-centered" or self-concerned. And it will certainly let you know who and what are really important to you.

Journal writing can make you grateful for the life you are living—with all its complexity.

It can make you laugh, seethe, cry, howl, rejoice.

It can bring to life your artist's soul.

It can make you honest.

It can give you a greater sense of choice about how you are living your life.

This is how Meredith describes her journal-writing life.

Meredith

66 I have been journal writing on and off for about 14 years; most writing seems to have coincided with trips overseas or other critical periods in my life. Recently (last 12 months) I have been pretty disciplined with keeping a journal. This coincided with a major shift in my personal life—my husband decided to leave our marriage for another woman. The process of getting 'stuff' out of my head was extremely important to me (and still is!!). Sometimes, particularly in the middle of the night, when I felt I couldn't call friends, my journal was there, waiting to 'listen' to me. Writing in my journal felt like a safe way to organize my thoughts so I could be in the processes of working out just what I wanted, where I was going, how I felt, and dealing with my grief.

Some of the entries are extremely brief; others stretch out into nine or 10 pages. I'm up to book number three over the last year! Sometimes the short entries relate to being very tired, and the gaps in the journal may coincide with trips away for work and being exhausted in the evenings and not giving it a priority in the mornings. Some of the longer entries were when I wasn't sleeping that well and I felt the need to free up my racing mind by writing.

Some of my really long entries are full of anger and despair, while others describe moments of moving on and beautiful experiences. The same goes for short entries. I recall one entry where I wrote, 'I am still cranky with ———.'

I do reread my journals, and that is a very powerful experience to read how much I have worked through and also to remind myself that even in the pits of my darkest moments, there was still beauty and even humor. Currently I am interested in seeing where I was 12 months ago or six months ago and to appreciate the process and my journey.❞

Your most creative self

The work of writing for me can be, or can be very close to, the simple job of *being*: by creative reflection and awareness to help life itself live in me.

—Thomas Merton

Journal writing offers an invaluable opportunity to deepen your creativity across all aspects of your life, not just writing. I feel so passionately about this: the stirring and developing of your creative abilities through journal writing. Creativity is key to feeling alive, to meeting situations freshly even when things are not going as brilliantly as you might want. It's key to doing things, thinking about events, facing life with some originality, using your senses—in your own way and style. And those benefits will emerge whether or not you write "well" in the conventional sense or believe you have "enough" or even "anything much" to say.

A creative moment brings energy with it. Laughing out loud, opening up to an "aha" moment, reading or writing something that wakes you up, looking at a stale problem with new eyes, creating something of beauty that may be no grander than a single white flower in a narrow glass vase, or setting a table with candles and polished stones beside each plate, or buying six cushions in shades of green, or bringing your own opinions to an otherwise dry report.

Writing something in your journal that is fresh, driven, authentic, observant, and deeply felt is also highly energizing and, at the same time, surprisingly calming.

Writing "well" is irrelevant here. So are concerns about perfect spelling or grammar or even ease with words. Ease with words—and with what those words are expressing—grows as your journal-writing experience deepens. I can guarantee this.

English novelist, critic, and journal writer Virginia Woolf was one of the greatest literary stylists of the twentieth century. Of her journal writing, however, she could say: "The rough and random style of it, often so ungrammatical, and crying for a word altered afflicted me somewhat.... Now I may add my little compliment to the effect that it has a slapdash and vigor and sometimes hits an unexpected bull's eye."

"Vigor" drives this journal extract from Jessica, who, I suspect, uses her journal—among other things—as a kind of circus "big top" where she can dazzle with wordplay for no one's delight but her own.

Jessica Perini: Journal extract

Sometimes I feel like I am dancing through life. My steps are practiced so that there is no more thought to them and I glide through the air like a ballerina on Prozac, kind of elegant but a little more bulky. And then I think something like "Wow, I'm dancing, I really am dancing, how wonderful." Then I trip and fall flat on my face, my dress goes everywhere, my pants show, and it becomes obvious I haven't shaved my legs. How awful. Sometimes human beings are like that: they get all happy and forget that they are pursuing happiness and for one second they experience bliss. Then they trip up and spend the rest of the time lamenting that second where they lost their peace of mind. (I just wrote an interesting typo there, instead of "peace" wrote "piece." Of course that would be a bit messy leaving pieces of your mind here and there, not to mention a health and safety catastrophe.)

From the first moments, and without pushing or trying, journal writing builds the spontaneity and intensity that a creative response to life demands. It also builds insight, courage, a sense of spaciousness, and humor. In return, it asks from you only tenacity and truthfulness.

Collage in words

It is impossible to say this too often: Journal writing is all about process, not outcome.

One page, ten pages; a page filled with words; a page listing words; a letter to a friend who died a year ago; slapdash dialogues; delicate haiku; a list of books you are reading; a prayer that inspires you; tickets from the first night of a play and a quick sketch—*all of that is journal writing.*

Putting the inside out

Writing a journal involves externalizing your thoughts, ideas, feelings, impressions, reactions, dreams, ideals, sorrows, yearnings, hopes, and experiences. Putting them down on the page, you shift the way you perceive and think about them.

You do this simply by writing down what is in your mind as freely as you can. You engage with your thoughts and feelings from the inside out. This process is very different from keeping those same thoughts in your mind and turning them over and over by worrying, ruminating, or daydreaming.

When we ruminate, our thoughts often seem to get less varied and more restricting. We can so easily feel trapped by those thoughts, even as we are struggling to get beyond them. Putting them out there, onto the pages of your journal, shifts the energy of those thoughts in a distinct and most helpful way. Writing something down, I often feel that I am "making room" inside my own mind so that new thoughts can arise or so that my mind can rest. And whenever I teach journal writing and talk about this idea of "making room," I can see smiles of recognition all around the room. "Yes," others are saying, "that's how it is for me, too."

At the same time, the process of journal writing gives you an invaluable measure of distance between yourself and your thoughts, which makes it so much easier to see what's really going on and how best to act—or not. Or what really matters—or doesn't. I cannot emphasize too strongly how helpful this is.

You can become curious about a complex situation rather than be overwhelmed by it.

You can find out what you really think and feel. You can find out what you want.

Sometimes this is dramatic, and you see something quite differently, or feel very differently about it, almost at the moment you are putting your words onto the page. At other times the processes of externalization are subtle and quite gradual. You come to see things freshly or with helpful distance over time and perhaps when you have written about them over many days or weeks.

Time is something else that journal writing gives you. As you observe your own life and the life around you with the eye of a journal writer, your perspective shifts and changes. *Rushing* matters less. *Discovering* becomes far more interesting.

Not just *useful*

Journal writing is not just *useful* any more than any other work of art is simply useful. Your journal writing may be far from artistic. Nevertheless, it expresses the same impulses that drive the creation of any artwork.

A sense of discovery drives any creative endeavor. In her richly thoughtful book *Eternity's Sunrise*, Marion Milner shares the idea of taking up journal writing to meet her own soul. She also wanted to improve her powers of concentration and discover her aim or purpose in life.

Milner writes: "I decided that in the diary I would try to put down what seemed to be the most important thing that happened each day and see if I could find out from that what it might be that I really wanted." To her surprise, "What turned up as most important was not at all what I had expected."

This kind of "surprise" is what happens when your journal writing goes beyond simple reporting. It wonderfully demonstrates the creative possibilities of journal writing for me. Because who is it that's surprising you? Yourself.

A whiteboard in miniature

When I was introducing the idea of journal writing in my book *Choosing Happiness*, I wanted to find a way to ensure that it would make sense to people more used to writing in linear ways—like company reports or strategic plans—than anything creative or subjective. What I came up with was an invitation to think about journal writing as a whiteboard in miniature.

Even the most "left-brained" thinkers use whiteboards or their equivalents to brainstorm, share ideas, identify what matters—and what doesn't. The same principles can be used in creative journal writing. Writing things down—and they don't need to be complete thoughts any more than they do when you are brainstorming in company—lets you "see" your thoughts in fresh ways. It also lets you get vital distance from them. It allows new thoughts to arise, new connections to be made. And it allows and anchors insights.

Journal writing is also a brilliant way not just to set goals (in all areas of your life) but also to refine and monitor them.

- ∿ What's already working here?
- ∿ Who is this "goal" pleasing?
- ∿ Could I look at the goal or the process more constructively or freshly? What would allow that?
- ∿ What keeps me on track?
- ∿ What mini goals am I setting and achieving?
- ∿ Am I enjoying the process or engaging with it wholeheartedly enough to enjoy it?
- ∿ What gems am I discovering as I go?

Capturing the patterns

Writing a journal allows you to see the *patterns* of your own thinking, emotions, and actions. (*Patterns* will include habits and routines: "ways of seeing" that are automatic rather than fresh, including asumptions and stale or static judgments as well as habitual emotional reactions that may not be useful or even appropriate.)

These patterns will emerge quite inevitably within a few weeks of journal writing. And the unfolding of these patterns will empower you, not least to see what you are giving time and attention to, where your thoughts are taking you, what emotions accompany your thoughts, what insights are available or needed, where changes may be needed.

The way these patterns emerge surprises almost everyone. Lara expresses this very clearly.

Lara

❝ I had no idea how little of my emotional energy and creativity went into my own life. It wasn't until I had been writing my journal for a few months that I really saw clearly how exclusively focused I was on other people's needs. That's a good thing, too, but I had left myself behind. I was looking at my own life through the prism of their needs only.

Journal writing has been like switching on a light for me. I could see what I needed for myself—and I could see how bringing myself back into the picture and feeding my own creativity and 'dream time' actually benefited my family and friends also. Even my attitude to work has changed. I'm more confident but actually far more easygoing. ❞

The world outside yourself

Journal writing is an unparalleled resource for putting your inner thoughts and feelings "out there" on the page. "Journal writing makes me whole," says Ros. "It's the glue that keeps me together." Just as crucially, though, journal writing lets you see what you are taking in from the world beyond yourself. Those patterns also matter.

We live in a world that is as complex as it is dynamic. Our interdependence with others and with the world beyond ourselves is a fact, not an option. We are surrounded by other people and countless nonhuman species, by made and natural objects of the most extraordinary variety, by every imaginable kind of sensual and intellectual stimulation. Things "happen" that are apparently outside and beyond us yet impact us on a moment-by-moment basis.

Observing which events and experiences actually come into your awareness and find their way into your journal writing will help make you much more actively aware of what underpins your life—and the ceaselessly dynamic relationship between your inner and outer worlds.

On the day the French people stormed the Bastille on July 14, 1789, Louis XVI wrote in his diary a single word: *"Rien!"* Nothing!

An empty page in your journal is an invitation. It is a door or window opening or falling away. It is a meeting place for inside and outside. It is a promise. All you need do is rise up to meet it.

❧

Free associations

One of the rewards of journal writing that I love most is giving myself the chance to receive the unsought and sometimes emotionally very powerful associations that come to mind *because journal writing makes space for them*. These are the associations that would never occur without first writing something down, first giving myself a prompt. (And I don't need to know in advance what the prompt is. For me, for Marion Milner, whom I quoted above, and for countless other journal writers, the prompt is sometimes, indeed often, at the far side of what I believe I am most caught up with.)

For example, as I wrote that final phrase in the section above, "rise up to meet it," in a very "journal-writing" way I was flooded with a vivid memory of sitting in my car with my daughter just a few months ago listening to the words of an old song that has recently been rereleased and made newly popular— "You raise me up…"—and how much we enjoyed listening to that together. We were in fact "raised up" by it. But then with no effort from me, I found myself remembering in a rush so many times when music has enchanted or sustained my children and me, or given us a lovely respite from thinking about more pressing or difficult things, as we sat in different cars travelling from one place to another through all the years of their growing up. In journal writing, linear time gives way to sensual time.

This is exactly how I would write in my own journal. Letting one sentence take me to the next. And sometimes not sentences at all. ("Tenors singing corny heavenly songs. Tender beautiful daughter, so loved. Gabriel making us laugh. Little kids in the old Volvo. Noisy kids—sometimes six in the car pool. Car filled with children. Life filled with children. Driving home from school across the Sydney Harbour Bridge. Music moving through everything. Forgetting what was hard. Gifted again by all that was good.")

Dieter's way of free associating is inspired by numbers. I was delighted when he sent me the following description, bouncing off from a speaking event I had done in his home city a year or so earlier. One of the reasons I am so pleased to have this, and to share it, is that I had never thought about numbers as being part of the creativity that journal writing could support. But that is simply because I myself am so word focused. Watch how the magic of associating through numbers works for Dieter. (And notice how apt it is that my mind gave me the "hint" to start that previous sentence with *Watch*. It wasn't until my fingers were typing the word and I saw it on the screen that I began to smile.)

Dieter

❝ You [Stephanie] didn't have a watch, but I helped you out, when it was 5:30 p.m. or was it 6:30? Well, to find the details, let's open my diary.

Quote: *Sat next to 'Bowden.' At first I sat behind him, then I saw man on his own, if I sat in this seat it's row 2, seat 4, Stephanie is nice, had no watch, I said: It's 6:30! (9 only to make it 693). Didn't stay after.*

As you can see, I am much of a numbers man. 24 and 693 mean something. That afternoon I had also been to the market and bought 8 tomatoes. The girl had said, 5 would make 1 kg, but I took 8, which came to 1,000G exactly. Next I saw a car, an MG sports car with rego plate MG, which represents 1,000 (M)(G)rams. Believe me, to think this one up would take a genius, but I just observed it with my own eyes, that's all.

It's a long story, happened on 10/18/05, no kidding.

Just like this morning, when I woke at 6:14 (I don't use alarm clocks anymore) and it was June 14 (6/14).

In the same way, I could open my diary at almost any day and find something magic.

Take the time I reset my odometer in my car. I was going to check how far I was driving that morning. When I looked at the odometer, at exactly 15.3 kilometers I passed No.1053 on Adelaide's South Road.

On 3/5 this year (still on the 3 & 5 magic) I was going for a short evening bicycle ride. About 2 kilometers from my house (in a street I don't very often cycle through) I found 3 ten-cent coins and one 5-cent coin within a few meters from each other.

Without writing in my diary, I would not remember the details of events. Many times as I write I discover more of this kind of magic—like on 4/11 this year, I just happened to write on page 114 in my diary. (On this occasion I had numbered the pages myself, because it was a ring-bound diary, and I did not want pages to go missing without record.) "

Here is a completely different example from a published journal written by Anaïs Nin. Her journals became her major creative work and were hugely popular with readers for many years. Yet hers is not the "right" way to free-associate; it is just her way. Your way may be different. And my hunch is that it may also be strikingly different on different days. Nin wrote: "I cannot remember what I saw in the mirror as a child....Perhaps a child, like a cat, is so much inside of himself that he does not see himself in the mirror. He sees a child....No reflections. Feelings. I can feel what I felt about my father's white mice...the taste of a burnt omelette my father made for us...the feel of the beach in Barcelona."

Mirror, child, cat, mice, omelette, beach: Free association—yours or Nin's—is highly instinctive and is often quite spontaneously prompted by something that stirs the senses. The origin of such an unlikely trail could be the smell of fresh coriander or an ancient iron bath, the dust that falls from books that have been stored, unstirred, the sound of a school bell in the distance, heavy rain on an unlined tin roof, a gray cat lying on a patchwork cushion, a note scrunched up at the back of a drawer, out-of-date currency, a prayer written in your own ten-year-old handwriting.

Your turn
━◆ *Free associations*

Wherever you are, right now, let your eyes or attention fall on something outside yourself.

It could be the sofa on which you are sitting. It could be a vase of flowers that a day ago were so fragrant and are now about ready to be thrown out. It could be the smell of dinner cooking. It could be the silence that you are suddenly "hearing." It could be the roar of traffic or the sound of someone talking on the phone in another room. It could be the toys that are littered across the floor. Or a story in the newspaper that you discarded this morning.

Whatever feels promising or engages you, choose that, then pick up your pen, open your journal or notebook, and simply let yourself write for at least ten minutes using what's engaged you as your jumping-off point. If you go off at a tangent at once, that's fine. If you keep coming back to the vase of flowers and how your uncle grew the most fragrant roses you have ever smelled...that's also fine.

The crucial thing is to keep writing for at least ten minutes, to incorporate your hesitations or obstructions in your actual writing ("This seems forced to me, but on the other hand my writing hand is still moving and so are my thoughts...") and to let your imagination and your senses off the leash. *Fly!*

My suggestion is to use this written form of free association very freely! And keep in mind that it is very different from ruminating *without* writing things down. When you are setting out on your journal-writing life, use free association as often as you can to increase your writing flexibility. Take yourself off the tracks of linear thinking and into the pathless spaces of creative thinking.

You may even want to free-associate on the idea of creative thinking, or the word *creative*, or the word *thinking*. The same simple principles apply: Surrender, write, and discover.

All the senses offer an astonishingly powerful direct route to memories. Perhaps smell is the most direct. Try this!

Your turn
✒ *Follow your nose*

AS YOU START
Wherever you are, something will have a distinctive smell. Or open the window and put your head outside. (Breathe in with your eyes closed.) Or check the fridge. Or take the elevator down to the ground floor and wait while people rush by.

Very soon someone will be carrying a take-out coffee, or will be wearing the same perfume your aunt did when she got involved with that amazing man from Peru; or a scooter will go by, belching foul air, and it will remind you of the time you were stranded in Sicily with your friend Jane without a passport.

Once you have identified a particular "smell" in your immediate environment, begin free-associating on your page. Write lists or complete sentences. Choose. Change.

CONTINUE WITH

Keep going until you have jumped "thoughts" or associations at least fifty times. (Well, thirty will do if you are happy with them!)

And why not also free-associate with the phrase "following instructions" or the phrase "being good"?

END WITH

Before you finish writing for the day, complete this sentence: "The most surprising association of all was…"

More on free-associating

You can play the free-association game with any one of your senses dominating: touch, taste, hearing, smell, sight. Once you give your mind permission to "play" in this way, free associating—making unbidden connections—will also quite naturally become part of your creative journal writing, providing your journal-writing life with depth and texture and all kinds of surprises.

Words themselves are stunning "jumping-off points" for free-associating. Start with some of the "big" words that resonate with meaning for almost all of us: God, place, parents, hope, friends, loved ones, peace of mind, justice, loneliness, confidence, purpose, death, values, desires, "enough," cravings, danger, loss, children, early, late, power, words, hope, money, health, siblings.

Allow yourself to jump from one connection to the next *without judging.*

Write down all your thoughts, and feel very free also to comment on the process as part of your journal writing, especially while it is happening. ("Was writing about danger quite happily when the word *synchronicity* swooped down, and I find myself wondering whether the kinds of coincidences that you might call synchronistic make this world safer or not, so now I guess I am writing about safety although I am very tempted to run away with the idea that Dad of all people was incredibly superstitious, and I remember one time when he...")

Whenever you have finished writing for the day, let your thoughts "rest."

In his example on pages 21–22, Dieter demonstrated the magic (and the synchronicity) he finds in numbers. I would add, never underestimate the power of words. As William Stafford wrote in *Writing the Australian Crawl*, "Working back and forth between experience and thought, writers have more than space and time can offer. They have the whole unexplored realm of human vision."

A "whole-brain" activity

Journal writing develops both your so-called right-brain strengths (lateral problem solving, intuitive, creative, emotional) and your so-called left-brain strengths (intellectual, sequential, rational, orderly).

My personal experience is that these functions are so inevitably integrated in journal writing that it becomes a true "whole-brain" experience. One minute you are writing something about your day that is "useful" to remember (left brain), then suddenly you are off, making an association that takes you in an unexpected direction (right brain). You may then write down a problem that you want to solve (left brain) and that you are prepared to leave to "cook" until you return to your journal in a day or two (right brain) when, with luck, your unconscious will have solved it for you! Yet before you finish for the day you make a quick "Must-do-tomorrow" list so that you don't have to think again about those tasks until the morning.

Even more excitingly, sometimes you find yourself writing about a "left-brain" rational aspect of your life—work, for example—with a "right-brain" creative/intuitive perspective. Or you may be rereading your journal to find the patterns, which would seem to be a rather "left-brain" activity, when actually you are "following your nose" in a delightfully "right-brain" kind of way and coming up with "patterns" far beyond those that initially interested you.

Good reasons not to write a journal?

Writing a journal is not essential. It is not going to get the house cleaned. It is not going to get children or chickens fed, lawns mowed, bills paid, or checkbooks balanced. It is not something that you would usually include in your résumé or mention to others to enhance their opinion of you.

It is extremely tempting to trivialize journal writing in your own mind, especially before it becomes part of your life. Or to tell yourself that you will write a journal when you have more time. Or to assume that you can give time to your journal only when everything that really "matters" is done. "The habits of a lifetime when everything else had to come before writing are not easily broken," warned writer Tillie Olson.

This is how Michele describes it.

Michele

❝❝ I find that journaling is a way of having an open dialogue with oneself. Talking openly with others about your life and what you are going through is one way of dealing with what is happening to your body and mind and spirituality. But with a journal the experience of communication becomes much more uncensored and, in a way, becomes a mechanism in understanding the way you think, feel and see which is much more empowering. At any time, in any place, you alone can help yourself with reflections and drawings that get to your heart and soul. 🙶🙶

Long-term journal writers know the benefits of journal writing. (And for many of them journal writing truly does become essential.) But when you are setting out on the journal-writing adventure, it can be very useful to meet some of the obstacles to journal writing right up-front and to discover for yourself how best to circumvent them.

"Only teenage girls write journals"

Teenage girls are often avid journal or diary writers—and for good reasons. Many of the journal writers who have contributed to this book began writing in their teenage years. That was my story, too. (Some dropped it for some years, then went back to it; others have maintained it as a lifetime commitment.) And when I teach journal writing there are always committed, insightful younger journal writers in the group.

The pity is that too many of us are persuaded to give up journal writing as we get older, often because we really do let ourselves become convinced that there are more important things to do or that we should be attentive only to other people's lives and not to our own. So journal writing gets sacrificed, *along with much of our creativity*. What also gets lost is a good deal of our sensitivity to the contours of our own unique existence.

Sometimes we also give up because our way of writing a journal is limited and eventually bores us. Recognizing that was a big incentive for me to open out journal writing through my classes and this book and to affirm it as a powerful and creative response to life and living.

Those who begin journal writing in adolescence—and they

may well be boys as well as girls—usually do so quite instinctively, discovering as they go how effectively it helps them to make sense of the outer world and their own complex and often conflicting inner emotions and impressions. They may also use it as a brilliant way to get "a handle on things": to gain a sense of perspective when events or emotions may otherwise feel overwhelming. They may love the sensuality and portability of it, especially if they otherwise spend much of their time working at a computer.

Like you, they probably find it empowering to discover what they think and feel. And to learn how inevitably even the most powerful moods and emotions give way to something else. (Life itself moves through us always, changing things.)

Here are two brief examples of teenage journal writing from Karen Horney, who grew up to become a famous pioneering psychoanalyst.

At age thirteen: "Today I got a bad mark for behaviour. To be honest, it makes no difference to me whatsoever. It was because I let another girl copy. Otherwise it's really great in school....It will soon be my birthday."

At age seventeen: "Everything in me is storming and surging and pressing for light that will resolve this confusion. I seem to myself like a skipper who leaps from his safe ship into the sea.... He doesn't know where he is going."

And who could resist the clarity and courage of perhaps the best-known teenage journal writer of all, Anne Frank: "I want to write, but more than that, I want to bring out all kinds of things that lie buried deep in my heart." Or this affirmation of life, as Anne lived in hiding, facing death: "Everyone has inside of him a piece of good news. The good news is that you don't know how great you can be! How much you can love! What you can accomplish! And what your potential is!"

Whatever our age, the discoveries that come from journal writing yield exceptional benefits. It's true that in adolescence people may sometimes be highly focused on emotional events. It's also true that when the world seems very black and white, they may find it difficult to look for or find the bigger and more optimistic picture, or even to see things from other people's points of view. But journal writing helps with that.

It helps us gain perspective and a bigger sense of life's vista. And because we are literally externalizing our most persistent thoughts on paper, it also helps us to stop returning to the same unproductive thoughts over and over again. That's truly liberating, however young or old we are and however experienced at creative journal writing we are.

"It's very strange," wrote Katherine Mansfield, New Zealand short-story genius and one of the best-known journal writers of all, "but the mere act of writing anything is a help. It seems to speed one on one's way."

Among the most exhilarating discoveries that any journal writer will make (that *you* will make) is that journal writing itself is infinitely flexible. It comes to meet you at whatever stage of life or maturity you have reached. Better yet, it can take you forward.

"Adults have better things to do"

Adults do, indeed, have many things to do, and it is very easy to go along with the view that journal writing should not be one of them. Nevertheless, most journal writers I have talked with or taught find that, without thinking about it very much and certainly without "trying," they have learned to allocate their time with more skill and sensitivity than before they were journal writers.

How? Why?

The habits of journal writing create a most interesting distance between you and your thoughts. Finding out that your thoughts are not inevitable and discovering that not only your thoughts but also your feelings change when you write your thoughts down, you can shift the emphasis, style, and content of your thinking. Experiencing your own powers of observation, coupled with a greater awareness *that you have choices,* increases your sense of self-mastery and inner stability. This is no small thing.

Journal writing also teaches reflection and brings focus. It gives you a heightened sense of what it means to be present, and it hones concentration. *It gives you room to know yourself in depth.*

"The mind is a mansion. But most of the time we are content to live in the lobby," writes William Michaels. This thought makes me laugh, and in the very same moment it makes me furious that we could be content with so little (or discontented, yet do so little about it).

Without some kind of training and practice in awareness, no matter how intelligent, motivated, or highly educated we may be, we tend to spend much of our time absent from the present moment, reacting to other people's cues without very much self-awareness or sense of choice. Things "happen"; the details pass us by. It's a bit like driving for hours, obeying all the traffic rules, but without noticing where you have actually been. Did you pass a giraffe ten minutes ago, or was it a gas station?

It is impossible to write a journal consistently and not become more intelligently reflective and more awake.

As your journal writing continues, this means that you become not only a more acute observer of your own life but also a more acute observer of *life.* Those twin capacities to observe and reflect give you inner balance, a greater sense of choice, and certainly a most welcome freedom from the experience of being buffeted and tossed about by events and emotions.

Here's how Candy sees it.

Candy

66 When I am in the process of actually writing about something, then I am usually totally absorbed in what I am doing. I am not thinking about it very consciously. I'm just getting it down. I am letting myself roll with it. But what I find fantastically useful is the space that exists between me and those emotions once I have got them down. I am noticing that it's a kind of relief to get things 'out there'—onto the page. That's unexpectedly true even about quite pleasurable things. I sometimes feel like I am clearing my inner decks ready for the next new moment.

I am definitely far more 'present,' moment by moment, since I have been journaling. I feel like I have greater curiosity, too, about my life. And I am certainly valuing it more. Where is it going next? Where am I going next? Whatever happens, I feel ready for it. 99

"Journal writing will make you monstrously self-absorbed"

Critics of journal writing (who have rarely tried journal writing themselves) usually begin and end their criticism by rattling your fears that journal writing will make you more or even unbearably self-absorbed. Their criticism—or simple lack of enthusiasm—will prick and hurt if it echoes the warnings of your own inner critic or pumps up your own self-doubt. So some warnings are in order.

There may be times when you will want to write in your journal more than anything else. You may want to write in your journal more than you want to watch television with your partner or fold laundry or review that crucial report for tomorrow's meeting. There may also be times when you are totally preoccupied by a most unexpected insight or revelation, especially one that comes to you like a brilliant flash after several weeks of ho-hum writing. There may be evenings on end when journal writing feels like a priority. And why not?

Enjoyment of your own creativity is an essential ingredient of journal writing. Indeed, greater enjoyment of your life is a perfectly reasonable expectation! So it is certainly possible that you might come to think rather better of yourself as your journal-writing life progresses. ("Did I write that amazing sentence? Was it sensible, prosaic me who caught, perfectly, the bliss of stepping into the ocean pool on a hot summer's day? Is that really my own witty/wise/accurate/perspicacious insight? Am I the sage who can make myself laugh a year after an event simply by reading what I wrote then in such a rush and without a moment's conscious judgment?")

What is not true, however, is that engaged, creative, expansive journal writing will make you more self-absorbed than you already are. In fact, chances are good that you will become significantly *less* self-absorbed, *more interested in the world around yourself,* and certainly more interesting as your journal writing enhances your skills of observation, concentration, and awareness.

Generally, the less sure of ourselves we are, the more self-focused and self-referential we will be. The more secure we are—and journal writing can support this—the easier it is to open up to what's around us, including a variety of other people's views and experiences. I love the way Naomi describes this enlarging of awareness.

Naomi

❝ I have been a journalist [such a nice way to describe "journal writer"!] since the age of seven or eight, but only when I read Julia Cameron's *The Artist's Way* was there an objective view of what the process might yield. I followed her precepts through the darkest hours of my adult life and drove myself almost nuts with boredom in the process. All the same, I remembered the adage 'Change takes place at glacial speed,' and persisted and persisted with the discipline of writing three pages a day, every day. This went on for two years, and then, magically, I began to witness a shift. My writing became less and less about myself and more and more a commentary on the outside world—even if it was only about the color of camellias outside the bedroom window, or the refraction of light off a crystal. Finally, my litany became a thanksgiving prayer, where every day I reminded myself to thank 'whoever' for my life, my gifts, and then, over time, my friends and family. I have never read back over those pages, knowing how deadly dull they were even for me! But there is no question that those Morning Pages, as Cameron calls them, became part of a daily meditation. Now I am writing again for the sheer joy of it as an essayist, aspiring journalist, and hopefully publishable novelist. Vive la journalism! ❞

Your journal-writing life will have its many stages and phases. Dull, predictable periods may be followed quite unexpectedly by times of intense writing, clusters of insights, glorious experiences of fluency, all of which halt again for no good reason until the whole cycle starts afresh.

Like every other aspect of journal writing, those cycles will, in their details, be unique to you. There may well be self-absorbed periods. There will also be periods when your observations take you far from home, but not so far that they become someone else's observations and not yours.

My view is that discovering what your observations are, what your reflections are, rather than living secondhand through the prism of other people's ideas and opinions, is one of the unrivaled joys of journal writing.

"Daydreaming had started me on the way," said writer Eudora Welty, "but writing, once I was truly in its grip, took me and shook me awake."

If there have to be some moments of self-absorption to discover that level of "awakeness," so be it. After all, journal writing potentially connects us to our deepest sense of self. It reveals us to ourselves. Yet the more deeply we delve, the less personal and more universal some of our discoveries will become.

At the place where the personal and universal meet, we feel most alive, even in times of sorrow. Your journal writing will let you experience that. In fact, your journal writing will facilitate and accomplish that.

Journal writing is a supremely effective way to engage with your own inner world *and* to engage more intimately and confidently with the world that is all around you and within you.

Privacy issues

Fears that other people will read what you are writing are very real for many people. It wasn't until I began teaching journal writing to large numbers of people that I fully understood this.

Some people are actually writing at least in part for others to read their journals, if not while they are living, then after they are dead. Family historians may well do this. For others, the act of journal writing is intensely personal and private.

Here are some ways to safeguard the sacred space of your journal writing:

~ Keep your journal in a safe and unobtrusive place. Don't make it easy for others to pry.

~ If you are writing something that is especially private—or that may be hurtful to someone else—consider writing it on separate sheets of paper rather than in your current journal. You may feel that you can throw those pages away once you have clarified your thoughts and feelings by writing about the issues. If you want to keep what you have written, or if you prefer to write directly in your journal, develop a private shorthand or coded method for yourself. Write very small and more illegibly than usual.

~ Speak to a friend or family member whom you can trust and give very clear instructions as to what you would like done with your journals should something happen to you.

- Don't offer to read sections to other people. Don't talk about your journal writing in enticing ways. Don't be too heavy or ostentatious about "going off to write in your journal." Your excitement about journal writing may be very real, but it will intrigue other people much less if you keep that to yourself.
- Write illegibly. I have quite reasonable handwriting in everyday life, but in my journal it shrinks and becomes far less legible than usual. This happened quite unconsciously, but I certainly see the benefits. I also use abbreviations that I learned decades ago through a system called speedwriting. You could easily devise your own. Some sentences in my journal could be read by others, but by no means all. When it comes to journal writing, I am with Kurt Weill: "I don't care about posterity. I am writing for today."

Anaïs Nin is reputed to have kept her journals in a safe-deposit box. You would still need to bequeath them to someone you could trust.

This is how Lyneve has dealt with some of those privacy issues that haunt most journal writers from time to time.

Lyneve

❝ I've always been a compulsive keeper of journals/diaries. It started in my teens, took a nosedive when I had children, except for one year when I made a valiant effort to document the daily events of my two children under two years!

When I divorced in the mid-1980s, keeping a daily journal was a good way for me to stay grounded. It was a safe way to express my inner feelings—without consequences! And what a collection of stories I have! Some of work successes, heaps about relationship disasters, and lots about my three children's journeys. I stopped writing daily some years ago and now just write about 'significant events.' And on the first day of the New Year I always write about 'the year that was' under the headings of family, work, love, and what I wish for the year ahead.

Journals are wonderful. I have a stash of them in a box in my cupboard. Sometimes I reread them, but as they are such an important part of me I just can't bring myself to get rid of them. So I've left a note in my Will papers for my children about my journals, as follows:

'For much of my life I have kept journals. These have been a sort of "stress management" to help me deal better with life's troubles. You are welcome to read these journals or destroy them—your choice. But if you do read them, you may be struck by the negativity, the honesty, and the struggles. Please temper your reactions with compassion and empathy. There have been many bumps along the way for me, but I truly believe that whatever happened did so for a reason—these were lessons I needed to learn.' 💬

Robbie has also thought about these issues of privacy. Her solution is different from those of most of the journal writers I have talked with, but it works for her, and certainly the commitment she has to journal writing, and the rewards she gets from it, are not diminished because her focus is entirely on journal writing in the present moment, not as something for posterity.

Robbie

66 Journaling is always a part of my daily spiritual practice. It's not a matter of getting motivated to do it; it's that *without* the journaling I'm not motivated to cope calmly, serenely, and wisely with the myriad things a day brings along!

A little tip I learned for writing the most difficult, painful, or private stuff—the kind of things that you almost can't bear to see in writing, or definitely don't want anyone to see (EVER!): Just write the first letter of each word; it's easy with practice. It's unreadable to anyone (including yourself) so you have absolute freedom and safety to bring anything into the light.

Keep or reread journals?

No way! I am not writing a book or an artwork! It's a conversation between me and God. I write and listen. He talks and listens. I use ordinary spiral-bound exercise books and bin them as soon as they are full. 99

A different view again is expressed by Helen, who had the very harsh experience of having her privacy violated.

Helen

66 When I started to write, I shared my home with a husband plus a teenage son & daughter. To keep my journals private I used to carry them around with me, but soon I had too many—talk about baggage! I bought a large sturdy gift box & a long length of wide ribbon— I could keep my writing under my bed in the box, wrapped with a big bow, knowing that if someone

wanted to read it they would have to make a very conscious decision to untie the ribbon & open the box. However, over time I have come to feel much less concerned about this aspect of journaling. Though my writing is mostly a private experience there is nothing I have written that I am ashamed of or would shrink away from. I don't feel there is a difference between what & how I write when I think it's for 'my eyes only' or if someone else might be reading it; I find I can be honest & authentic either way. I write both by hand & on the computer. A few years ago my marriage broke down & my husband moved out. During a very acrimonious divorce & settlement I learned he had printed out & kept some of my private writing. Though I would not change a word of what I'd written I felt it was a gross violation of my privacy especially since at any time prior to the separation, if given the opportunity, I would have gladly shared with him any of my thoughts or feelings.

The last half dozen years have been an intense, fraught & painful time; however, my writing has brought immense solace. My writing imbues my inner world with a richness that was previously absent. Journal & journey—for me they go hand in hand. 🙶🙶

♪

At ease

Anaïs Nin made an art form out of her journal writing. Yet she commented on it very simply: "In the journal I am at ease." As you progress with your own journal writing, you will see for yourself how your moods and attitudes affect not only what you write but also how you interpret what you have written. Those variations alone will tell you a great deal about yourself.

There will be times when you reread something you regarded as "nothing much" or as dull while you were writing it, if you thought about it at all, and now find something in it that seems astonishingly helpful or new. (I am repeatedly amazed—in fact, I am almost ashamed at how much I have forgotten any time I reread old journal entries.)

Perhaps you can see how persistently you have been avoiding a key issue or how you've been writing about it from a limited and unhelpful perspective only. Perhaps a pattern that is quite new to you emerges. Perhaps you notice that it is possible to move on somewhat from an old grief or from a reworking of sorrow or regret. Perhaps you find a little humor in what had previously been a grim situation. Perhaps you suddenly sense a new possibility in what had appeared to be a closed story.

In all kinds of ways, journal writing will expand your choices, intensify your strengths and your knowledge of those strengths, and genuinely support you. But you do need to pay it regular attention.

Like any other intimate relationship, journal writing gives back in direct proportion to what you bring to it. It certainly requires a reasonable level of commitment from you if it is to flourish beyond the rewards of simply recording (and recalling) events.

Journal writing also requires you to be truthful and trusting of the writing process even through flat or bleak periods. In return, however, journal writing will give you a degree of clarity and insight that really cannot be acquired any other way. (It offers something quite different from conversation with another person, or from an interior conversation with yourself as you turn your thoughts over and over without putting them down on paper.)

A degree of fidelity is needed, yet there is something delightfully spontaneous and unstructured about journal writing. And I love that! There's no need to know exactly what you want to write about before starting. Nor is there any need to justify taking time for journal writing by finding something worthwhile to write about. In fact, the opposite is true. If you already knew just what you wanted to write, there would be no need to do so.

I very much like the way that Michele captures the depth of journal writing. And how journal writing can support you during protracted challenging periods.

Michele

❝ I am an artist and have been a journal writer for about 6 years, writing or drawing nearly every day. When I was 15 [she is now 29] I was diagnosed with Crohn's disease, which at the time only affected me like any other piece of information that is given to you as a teenager—mild indifference!

As an artist I have always had a love for collecting ideas and images in art diaries, but the process was always quite detached, never delving further into my collective conscious or unconscious. That was until my Crohn's disease started to affect my whole being! I began to realize, while living away from home, that so many parts of my life were changing and I needed a way of collecting all these experiences and changing perspectives.

I can now safely say that I could not live without my journal, which I carry with me wherever I go. I look back and reread past entries to understand past reflections and to look back at old dreams with fresh eyes. Working to understand my disease and myself, I am always trying to find new ways of improving my life…may it be hypnotherapy, meditation, a new book of theories, or an artist's work. By journaling through each of these new experiences I find that I am positively engaging and documenting my thoughts as I grow to understand what makes *me*. **"**

Journal writing is not about "getting the job done." It's not about writing more or more elegantly. It is about understanding better your own precious and complex existence as well as the world around you.

A sense of being increasingly in tune with your own existence is the unbeatable reward that journal writing offers. You will benefit, and so will everyone and everything that's in your life.

Your turn
➤ *Let the clock stop*

TRY THIS

Write down, thinking at whatever pace suits you best, exactly what you would do (or not do), begin, achieve, or complete if the clock stopped. Or if time no longer mattered.

When you come back to this exercise, write down all your associations with time, and then repeat the first part of the exercise.

Any changes?

A line of words

When you write, you lay out
a line of words.... Soon you find
yourself deep in new territory.

—Annie Dillard, *The Writing Life*

Free to be creative

Creativity—better than fame and fortune

Many things are far better than fame or fortune.

Love is one of them. Living creatively is another.

Living creatively means tuning in to all your senses and *really* knowing what's going on.

It means making quirky connections and seeking out inspiration, beauty, humor, tenderness, and absurdity.

It means liking the subtle as well as the magnificent.

It means valuing your own experiences and making something of them.

Creativity may be expressed through great works of art. But it can also be a way of living that is open, spirited, engaged, eager, curious, and uplifting.

Start here. Or there.

Journal writing is one of the rare forms of writing in which freedom of form and content support each other magically. You may want to go straight into writing about events ("Joe sick. Couldn't see Madeleine. No rain again"). That's fine. Though I want to say at once that creative journal writing can offer much more.

See how those facts fill out when they are written with a more creative "eye," and mixed with care and feeling:

"Made me very sad to see how ill Joe is this time. He's losing energy—one too many struggles. But we still managed to laugh uproariously when his tray of ghastly hospital food arrived. "Food for the particularly pale, wouldn't you say?" said my darling Joe. I'll take more food with me next time. I didn't get to see Madeleine, but that felt like something I could safely leave aside. She is so busy anyway and is very understanding. I'd like to catch up with her about the visit to Hawaii. Sits like heaven in my mind. No rain again, and the birds are circling for water as much as for food."

Creative journal writing, which usually takes very little extra time, can give you the tools and the confidence to record *and* reflect, to move between the outer and the inner, to develop creativity and spontaneity, to *pause*, fruitfully. In the next few chapters, that will be our focus.

We will come to the recording of facts; that's important, too. My experience is, however, that if journal writers limber up with some creative exercises, especially those that take them out of their comfort zone, when they come to the recording of "facts" that, too, will happen in a more dynamic and rewarding way.

Here is how a commitment to journal writing has supported Jessica, and enlarged and enhanced her world as she has moved with tremendous courage from being imprisoned by agoraphobia to being able to go out into the world again, cautiously, but with increasingly fewer limitations. I have read her entry a number of times, each time newly awed by her words, "I can see 'me' when I write…I can hear my true voice." Could there be greater testimony to this unsung art?

Jessica

❝❝ Journal writing saved me from myself. This is no exaggeration; I'm not spinning a yarn or telling a tall one. There was a time in my life before email contacts with the outside world. Before I could pick up the phone and ask for help, thinking that if I did, a friend might ask me to leave the house. A time when even with a fire engine outside and our building alarm blazing, I decided that if the apartments burned down I would stay and smoulder. Death was more comforting than the thought of leaving the house.

On a day just like any other—the shaking constant, my brain in a fog—I saw a small bird just outside on the balcony. It was a wood pigeon, flapping and frantically banging its little body against the glass. It was so frightened that it couldn't see that just below was a gap it could easily fly through. And a meter above that was free air where the balcony ended. If it could calm down enough it would be able to either squeeze under the balcony rail or fly over it.

'Calm down little birdy. Calm down,' I whispered. 'If you just calm down you'll see there's a way out.' And then I heard myself. Calm down. All I have to do is calm down. It was a revelation, so simple yet earth shattering. Could *I* be causing this shaking? Could *I* possibly have some control? Was this bird sent as a message from God? I had to record the moment for posterity. I had to hold on to this lesson.

And so, shaking, agoraphobic, and intensely depressed, I scrawled the first words. Then more. Pages and pages of thoughts and feelings fell out of me. I didn't care if anyone saw them. I felt this exhaustive shaking would last until I died; I could draw no other conclusion. But something strange happened: the more I wrote the more legible my writing became. It wasn't just from the practice; it was because I was switching to another part of my brain, a part not associated with my central nervous system. A logical part. And there I learned I had a small element of control. That tiny window of control led to others: meditation, nutrition, exercise. The shaking diminished.

To this day, I write and write. Usually not for publication or prestige but because I can see 'me' when I write. I can see my spirit, my logical mind, and my talents. I can hear my true voice. I really don't care who sees my writing, because they will see me. And if they like me, that's great. If they don't, that's no drama either. "

Forget school

It is possible that your capacity to express yourself freely may have been sorely inhibited by the many years you spent at school. *Forget school.* As the brilliant short-story writer Grace Paley put it, "I was a fantastic student until ten, and then my mind began to wander." If the way you write your journal satisfies you, then it is perfect. This book is not about writing *better*; it is about writing more *freely*.

Journal writing—and I will say this often throughout this book—focuses on process, not goals. It is about waking up to *now*, even when what you are writing about stretches you forward or backward from now. Just as gloriously, however you write and whatever you write is beyond the reach of mundane judgments like "perfect" or "imperfect." It is what it is, nothing more.

Let yourself off the hook of those limiting judgments, in your own private journal at least; it will help you write more freely. It will also help you to become less judgmental and critical of other people and generally less judgmental and more supportive of yourself.

This is what counts

In journal writing, it's the energizing qualities that count: passion, sensuality, truthfulness, compassion, curiosity, insight, creativity, spontaneity, artistry, and delight.

Spelling, grammar, neat handwriting, a sense of order, chronology or completion—none of these matter much at all when it comes to journal writing.

Choosing your journal

Choosing your first or next journal (and all your subsequent ones) is itself very much part of the creative journal-writing experience. While I was writing this book, I spent a wonderful hour in a specialty shop in my home city of Sydney with the woman in charge describing to me in loving detail which of the expensive, exquisite journals in her shop went primarily to young men ("They love the artistry of the handmade leather-bound journals as a contrast to their lives with computers"), which went to older men ("Elegant, softest leather wrappings of all"), which to older women ("The smallest—and the largest"), and which ones were seized upon with love by younger women ("Marbled, colored, and textured—somewhat ornate").

What I couldn't help noticing was that as she talked and as we moved around her small, elegant shop together, we were not just talking; we were touching, handling, sniffing, bending, squashing, delighting in the sheer beauty of these gorgeous products. Although—and I rush to say this—I have also written in the plainest of plain journals or even in cheap school exercise books without significantly affecting what I am writing or what I am concerned with.

This is how Lisa described the journals that have themselves been so much part of the "story" of journal writing for her.

Lisa

❝ My first lovely Corban & Blair journal was a long-neglected gift to myself and a permission to write, so the money actually made me feel more empowered to use it often and well!

Over the years I have often salivated over expensive books and have been honored to receive several spectacular ones as gifts from friends. One was covered in an old Indian sari and another in vivid yellow Vietnamese silk. Sigh. They excite so many senses at once! However, I have found that many of these more exotic species use handmade, untrimmed paper, and being an old-fashioned ink girl (fountain pens and only fountain pens), these books have not made the best journals as the luscious paper soaks up the ink into most interesting-looking blobs!

While working in a bookshop for a few years I grabbed hold of several 'anything' books (at a bargain $1.99 each) with hard board covers and wonderfully psychedelic patterns, which have been my standard for several years…but I am always on the lookout for more! ❞

Your turn
➻ Paper, pens, paints, promises

AS YOU START

Make a list of what will support you in your creative journal-writing life. In fact, make a *slow* list of what will support you. Luxuriate in your choices.

Start with what you need to buy. New pens? A new journal—what kind? Blank pages? Pages with lines? Something portable? Something that is unobtrusive and won't attract others' curiosity? Something outrageously luxurious and beautiful? Additional paper if you want to draw sketches or write when you are away from your journal? What kind of paper? Different colors for different moods?

What about paints or crayons? Will they be part of your journal-writing life? And where will you keep your journal-writing supports?

What about wrapping your journal in a silk cloth, creating a small ritual as you unwrap then rewrap at the beginning and end of each journal-writing session?

Decide, too, where you will sit to write your journal; how you will ensure quiet and privacy; what time of the day or evening will work best for you.

Write all of that down.

CONTINUE WITH

If you notice any inner commentary as you make your lists—and daydream about what your purchases will allow—write that down also. ("Am I kidding myself that I would write differently with a fountain pen?…Only one way to find out.")

END WITH

Create, in the pages of your journal, a brief promise to yourself that you will support your journal writing by purchasing what you most want.

Some practical suggestions

 Write in your journal regularly. Even a few minutes' writing on a busy day makes a difference. It helps keep you centred. It can calm you and even "create time." Writing reasonably regularly also gives invaluable continuity to your discoveries.

Combine the familiar with the unfamiliar. You may already be used to recording events or writing highly reflective journals. Whatever you are currently doing, there is no reason to stop, but do also try some of the exercises that appear in these pages. They will add to your repertoire of skills, increase your options, and with luck will broaden your vision.

Keep your journal where no one else will read it. You may want to share some of your insights or discoveries at some point, but don't be too eager to do so. Journal writing is, above everything, a personal process of self-discovery best done free even from the idea that someone else may be looking over your shoulder or observing the process. Don't leave your journal around to be read "by accident."

It is possible to be a computer-journal writer! Perhaps you feel that you must write your journal on the computer so that you can get your thoughts down fast enough, but I would suggest that you at least experiment with handwriting. For many journal writers this increases the sense of intimacy and makes a clear differentiation between the writing they do for work or for more public consumption and their creative journaling. Apart from anything else, your handwriting tells its own stories. Handwriting also makes your journal writing more personal. And there is a sensuality to the experience of your hand moving across a page in tune with your thoughts that itself can seem increasingly valuable.

Use a pen that flows smoothly and feels totally comfortable in your hand. Use several colors if you prefer. Free your creativity. Enjoy the freshness of mind and hand using pen and paper. In this computer age, that is an increasingly rare treat.

Choose your journals lovingly. Buy a journal that suits you and your particular needs. Treat yourself. I like large journals with creamy blank pages, but there have been times when I highly valued portability and some of my best journal writing—in the sense of most faithful, detailed, and rewarding—was done in small Chinese notebooks with thin paper and embroidered covers. Even your choice of journal tells a story and is worth writing about.

Keep extra pages of high-quality paper that you can fold into your more formal journal. Some of the exercises in this book will become part of your main journal, and you may want to do them a number of times. Don't limit yourself. I also find that most of my journals have inserted pages that I have scribbled when I have had some spare moments, old envelopes with notes, postcards, tickets, and other very precious memorabilia placed between pages. If I have a "journal-writing moment" when I am far from my journal I certainly don't want to waste it.

"Journal writing" includes and encourages every possible means of self-expression. If you want to draw or respond to an idea or situation by writing a short story or a poem, don't hesitate. Many literary writers have been committed diary or journal writers. In one of the most famous published journals, that of Katherine Mansfield, there are drafts of letters, fragments of short stories, circling of ideas, inner arguments, sublime insights, and the most ordinary noting of events ("J [Mansfield's husband] went to town. I worked a little—chased the fowls").

Journal writing *is* your teacher

Exercises are the key to freer and more creative journal writing. I am sharing many with you throughout this book. However, it's your own experience of these exercises that will allow your creativity to come alive. *The exercises themselves will be your teacher.* They will give you greater flexibility and skill as a journal writer. They will also give you insights that you may not get through even the most sensitive recording of events.

Here Maggie describes the way her journal-writing experience has grown.

Maggie

❝I saw my usual journal writing, which was generally in response to everyday events, as a separate style of writing to the entries I kept as a result of working through the creative exercises in *Living Words* [Dowrick's earlier journal-writing book]. In fact, I kept two separate journals as I didn't want to actually write in *Living Words*, although there was space to do so. I did note that I found it easy to write because, at the time, I was on leave. I know that I would not have been able to devote the time to *Living Words* if I had been at work.

My usual journal writing came as a response to events and the feelings and thoughts that came as a result of those events. It happened when I needed to pour out my thoughts. This writing just poured onto the paper.

In contrast, when responding to the prompts, I explored my own thoughts and beliefs about myself and my relationships with others much more deeply. This led me to view events in my life from a different perspective. The prompts took me back to experiences that would not have been a focus in my usual journal writing. This writing didn't just pour onto the page. It often came after carefully considered thought.

Though I didn't consciously make changes as a result of the thoughts that arose from my writing, I think the writing confirmed for me the places where changes were needed."

Neville's experience is also interesting, not least because he used his resistance to the very idea of exercises as the "key" to unlock information about himself.

Neville

"Writing exercises were anathema to me. Even when I tried I couldn't get past the idea of something set for homework by a teacher. I felt irritated even at the thought of them. On the other hand, I have been a careful journal writer for a good part of my life, and I could see that there was a certain element of stuckness in what I was writing and how I was approaching my journal.

The idea of 'whiteboarding' [from *Choosing Happiness*] was a breakthrough for me. In the early days of doing some exercises I don't think I ever wrote a complete sentence much less a totally completed thought. I am your classic tidy-mind obsessive, but I got to really like making wild lists that would occasionally end with a short insight, heavily underlined by me! Then I wrote out some of those insights onto cards. I felt boosted by that too. In fact, maybe those insights were more rewarding for me than the increase in creativity which I do recognize has also come about. The other thing that has come about is that I have grown to love words more, the more I have played the 'association' game and 'spin the question.' I look up quotation sites on the Internet now for fun and have even bought a couple of poetry anthologies, again to copy out poems or just a single line that I like.

The best result for me is that I can now recognize when I am holding myself back from a pleasure because of passé associations, not least of which was a fear that I didn't have a creative bone in me. Wrong! I am delighted to say. 🙶🙶

Reporting on your day

Trust that you can combine writing exercises like these with whatever style or format you are already using in your journal writing.

If you are keen to start or to continue to record details of your day as the main focus of your journal writing, do that confidently.

The creative journal-writing exercises this book offers will enhance whatever writing you are already doing.

- ∼ The exercises will build on what you already know.
- ∼ They will help you increase the self-knowledge and self-awareness you already have.
- ∼ They will allow you to revel in your own curiosity and observational skills.
- ∼ They will increase your writing confidence.
- ∼ They will reshape your version of a "comfort zone."
- ∼ They will give you pleasure.

Weaving the strands

As your confidence develops you may find that you are keeping several "strands" of journal writing going simultaneously. You may, for example, be spending time on these creative exercises while also tracking on a daily basis what's going on for you personally and occasionally dropping in a comment about a book you have read, a dinner you have cooked, a play you have seen, or a novel you plan to write!

Enjoy that. Carey's remarks about how her journal writing has freed her from linear thinking (even about how journal writing "should" be done) will strike a chord with many other journal writers.

Carey

66 As a lawyer, I have to be super-organized. I thought that I would write my journal in the same kind of way, but actually if I look at it now, a year later, it's a riot! I write with different-colored pens according to my mood. I print some sections and hand-write others. I draw in odd corners. I do follow themes through, but I am also always going back to things that I half-thought I had finished with. I see journal writing as an antilinear process, which is pretty radical for me. That certainly makes it far more enjoyable than I expected. It's as far from my experience of study and work as it could possibly be. **99**

Your turn
●← *First pages*

AS YOU START

Support the first moments of each new day's journal writing. Make them fresh and specific. Note the date and time, and add some details. Describe where you are sitting to write, or something about your physical environment. ("I am on the wooden bench in the garden today and am aware how lovely it is to look at the leaves for their own beauty rather than thinking about sweeping them up. That's what I need more time for: looking at leaves.")

Note what emotions are already bubbling up.

Be aware of what's going on in your body. ("Poor old neck. A few stretches feel terrific.")

CONTINUE WITH

Describe in detail how you feel about embarking on this journal-writing adventure. You will find your current reflections are of real interest to you as your journal-writing life continues.

If you are already a journal writer, explore what it means to you to enter a new phase in your journal-writing life. Was it the promise of *creative* journal writing that aroused your interest in this book?

Whether you are a new or practiced journal writer, ask yourself what you most want your journal writing to give you at this moment in your life. Write those possibilities down, as a promise to yourself.

What does the specific promise of "creative journal writing" mean to you?

GENERAL ENCOURAGEMENT

Spend as long as you want on any question or prompt.

Return to it until you feel completely satisfied.

Don't edit or rewrite as you go.

If you find yourself "judging," note that and move on.

If you are stuck, simply write about that—and out the other side.

Write for about twenty minutes, or longer if you have time and interest.

END WITH

Finish by taking a few moments to decide what insight has emerged that pleases you most.

Note that, and add a comment if you feel it's needed.

When you have finished, let your thoughts "rest."

Free writing

One of the greatest gifts that you can bring to your journal writing is your own inward permission to write freely.

What do I mean by this?

Writing without judging, comparing, and censoring is part of it. What also counts is pushing through, pushing on: continuing to write when you don't know what's coming next and especially when you feel your own resistances gathering in a mob to mock you.

A contract with yourself is needed in order to write freely: "I will write for at least twenty minutes." If, during that time, you find yourself with "nothing to say," *you write about that.* You describe what it is like to have nothing to say. Or you remember all the other times you had nothing to say. Or you ask the journal for help so that you can find out more about nothing (and we will look much more closely at the rich topic of "nothing" a little later in the book).

Addressing your journal directly can be surprisingly helpful. This is because your journal is standing in for your own deepest self. ("Dear Journal, I seem to be having a hard time taking seriously the idea that in spite of my crowded days and cluttered mind I could possibly have anything to say so I guess I am just going to have to go to the end of the highest diving board, hold my nose, and shut my eyes, and jump off…")

Because it is bringing your attention into the present moment, it is also freeing to describe on the page how your body feels, or even what you are observing about your handwriting, if your imagination seems to have stalled. What you don't do is stop until (at least) time is up.

Why am I urging you to push forward in this way? Because it is the absolutely key, essential method for you to learn to go deeper, wider, bigger than the thoughts that *generally occupy or preoccupy your mind*. Those thoughts are well known to you. Journal writing can give you more. However, it can only give you more if you are prepared to loosen up a little, persist, and invest in writing freely.

The other side of boredom

Sometimes you will have only a few minutes to write in your journal. *Take them.*

When you have more time, and especially when you are exploring one of the exercises, make a promise to yourself that you will write for at least twenty minutes. (The outer limit is up to you.) This gives you a chance to defy your boredom, to go beyond your hesitations and well-worn thoughts to see what's on the other side.

The key is to continue writing, commenting on how your body feels or the very feelings that are preoccupying or distracting you.

Trust the process.

Free writing is the life force of creative journal writing. The principles of free writing will apply in almost all the exercises offered in this book. This is also the way that I hope you will write your more "factual" accounts of daily life. And when you have practiced it a little in some exercises it will come to seem a very natural and unself-conscious way of writing that also, quite wonderfully, brings you thoroughly into the present moment even when what you are writing about is something from long ago in your past.

Your turn
New beginnings

I love the outsets, despite the fear and uncertainty
that attach to all beginnings.... I have already
begun a thousand lives this way.

—Rainer Maria Rilke, *Diaries of a Young Poet*

AS YOU START

Support the first moments of each new day's journal writing.
Make them fresh and specific. Note the date and time, and
add some details.

Note what emotions are already bubbling up.

Be aware of what's going on in your body.

CONTINUE WITH

What are your associations with new beginnings? Write them
down. (A list of words is fine and often a good way to start.)

Then "branch out," allowing your mind to make easy
associations to those first associations. ("New term. New
beginnings. Feeling like I am opening up to new knowledge.
Loved the start of a school year, at least until the last couple
of years when the pressure grew. Life now seems to be one
continuous "term." This beginning feels like a challenge.
Am I up to it? *Bracing* is the word that comes to mind!
*Em*bracing, too. Good to start on a new page, literally and
figuratively.")

Now choose one or more from the prompts that follow.
Find a new beginning from each of the decades of your life.
Take your time with this. You may need to return to this

same theme over several days or weeks until you see clearly which "beginnings" mattered most.

What do these "new beginnings" have in common?

Has the experience of beginning something new changed much over those years? Describe those changes in detail.

Are you judging yourself already? Putting obstacles in the way? Write those observations down. Once you see them, you can step around them.

GENERAL ENCOURAGEMENT

Whenever you feel stuck, just return to the idea of "new beginnings" and let your own internal associations prompt you. ("Love being an 'old hand.' Hate looking around the room and knowing no one. Yet when I first moved to Adelaide…")

Or write about being stuck.

Or notice and write about what's going on with your body. ("Am very relaxed. Headache gone. Pins & needles in toes but felt quite nice.")

Write for at least twenty minutes.

Don't edit or rewrite.

END WITH

Finish by completing this sentence: "The most unexpected thing I have discovered about new beginnings today is…"

Don't reread immediately.

Let your thoughts "rest."

Risking and writing

You won't come to journal writing without some preconceptions about it. And you probably won't come either without some deep wishes, even desires about what journal writing might yield up for you. The exercises that immediately follow give you a chance to explore some of that.

You may be doing these exercises while also running a parallel stream of journal writing about events and impressions: what's happening right now and to whom, and what you feel about it. That's fine. Each of these exercises has a double purpose: to find out where the topic is taking you and to stretch and encourage your observant self.

They will also show you how, by actively engaging with your own thoughts and experiences through your journal writing, far more of real interest will emerge for you than would ever be possible if you were simply reading a book, without also engaging, risking, and writing.

Your turn
"My associations with journal writing are..."

AS YOU START
Each time you open to a new page, start by noting the day and time of writing as well as some detail about where you are

physically. ("I have never written starting at midnight before, but tonight—or is it morning?—it feels perfect. When I put the two huge plastic rubbish bins out on the street, I had enough sense to pause and look up at the sky, where I was astounded for the millionth time in my life by the awesome sight of the faithful moon and more stars than I have seen for weeks. Coming in, I couldn't wait to grab this journal and...")

Notice (and note) what's going on in your body.

CONTINUE WITH

You may want to respond to one or several of the prompts below. Take a minimum of twenty minutes to write. The outer limit is up to you. Don't hesitate to come back to the same question over many days or journal-writing sessions.

Notice what questions you are avoiding. *Risk them.*

If you bought this book on journal writing for yourself, what was running through your mind at that moment of choice and purchase? If someone else gave it to you, what did you feel at the moment of receiving it?

What are your associations with journal writing, the words that most quickly spring to mind? Develop those thoughts. Associations with associations?

What are your first thoughts about journal writers? Jot down the words that most quickly spring to mind. Develop those thoughts.

What published journals, if any, have inspired you? If not journal writers, what else has inspired you?

What are your experiences more generally of being inspired or tenacious (choosing to stick with an activity whether or not you feel inspired)?

What areas of your life most urgently need your journal-writing attention?

Are there any particular emotions that you want to explore? Are there any situations where you feel stuck or even hopeless?

If you were to think of your journal as a friend (and you can), what special qualities will this friend have?

What talents/values/strengths do *you* have that journal writing might help you to develop?

What is the biggest possible wish that you could have for your creative journal-writing life?

Write for at least twenty minutes.

No stopping to edit or rewrite.

END WITH

Whichever prompt you chose, finish by completing this sentence: "The most unexpected thing I have discovered today is…"

Don't judge whether what you are writing is worth your time. (*Retire* the judge.)

Don't reread immediately.

Let your thoughts "rest."

More on motivation

The stories in this book reveal a great deal about each journal writer's motivation. As inspiring as they are, however, what will accelerate your own writing most successfully is understanding your own motivation to keep and sustain your journal writing.

Your turn
This journal-writing adventure

AS YOU START

Note the day and time, and something specific about your physical environment. ("It's another Saturday night, and here I am writing in my journal while the whole world is out on a date. Although not the people next door who are already playing their terrible music full blast. Can't complain though as they are great neighbors in other ways. I could ring one of my friends for a chat, but perhaps writing in my journal is what I choose to be doing. Am I a sad sack? Who cares.")

Note what emotions are already bubbling up.

Notice and note what's going on in your body.

CONTINUE WITH

Write a string of adjectives to describe this inner voyage: *scary, exhilarating, unsure, maddening.* When you feel as though you have run out, close your eyes, go "inside," and wait until more words occur to you. When something feels "right," circle that word. If you want to, write about your associations with that single word.

Write a letter to your journal ("Dear Journal…"), expressing your hopes and dreams for journal writing, then for self-discovery ("I have always wanted to be wise, to see things more clearly…"). Many great journal writers, including Anne Frank, have written to their journal in this way. The journal is simply a vehicle for your inner wise self.

Write out your thoughts and feelings about keeping secrets, even from yourself.

GENERAL ENCOURAGEMENT

Write for at least twenty minutes without giving up.

If you feel lost, just describe what's going on in the present moment. That will fire you up straight away.

Don't edit or rewrite.

Don't reread immediately.

Let your thoughts "rest."

Marion Milner (who also wrote as Joanna Field) is famous not only for her journal writing but also for her careful, highly analytic observations of the sometimes subterranean processes of journal writing. Her style of writing, and especially her detached analysis, may not instantly appeal to many contemporary readers, but she does offer some gems of insight in each of her three books about what journal writing gives and allows.

In *A Life of One's Own* she writes: "I had set out to try and observe moments of happiness and find out what they depended on.… The act of looking was somehow a force in itself which changed my whole being.… When I was living blindly I was pulled this way and that by all manner of different wants, but when I stopped to look at them their clamour died down."

Actor and director Richard E. Grant is also a journal writer. He drew on his own story for his film *Wah-Wah* and says: "I started keeping a diary when I was a boy in Swaziland and I saw my mother commit adultery with my father's best friend. I took refuge in writing....I still keep a diary. I think if you don't believe in God, writing is the equivalent of meditation. It's taking stock at the end of every day."

Understanding at least something about your motivation for writing your journal will be a tremendous support when it comes to sustaining your journal writing, especially through periods when it feels somewhat flat or forced. There is another side here, too. In the actual writing of your journal, your motivation will emerge almost inevitably. You will begin to see in black-and-white what your priorities are, your obsessions, your limitations, your joys. Here is a glimpse of Sue's many years' experience of journal writing and what it has brought her.

Sue

❝I have kept a journal on and off for a long time now. Probably since about 1984. I said to myself that I wanted to start to 'keep a daily record of my thoughts.' I was at a transition in my life with the beginning of my third pregnancy and serious morning sickness, and I was not able to work anymore, just too tired, I think. So I guess I decided to quit working and give in to the messages that my body was sending me. The beginning steps of conscious living and wisdom on my part, I think. I have looked back at my writing a few times and it is amazing to look at my own development over the past 20+ years!

It seems that I have changed my tactics depending on the latest fad that has been around, after the start of a kind of 'normal narrative' in 1984.

I went to a 'gratitude journal' for a few years, and that tells me something about what I have been happy about during those times but not nearly as much as the written narratives.

Around the year 2000, I then seemed to move to more of a prayer journal, speaking to God and thanking the Divine for things and asking for assistance with very difficult problems with our son. I was praying a lot (in desperation a lot of the time) as well as writing a prayer journal. I still pray silently, and my journal writing is now just peppered with prayers where I see fit to put them in, it seems. Being from a traditional Catholic-school upbringing, I still know a great repertoire of memorized prayers and like to use new ones as well as simply talking to God.

Regardless of the method that I have used, the same themes that arise as issues in my life have always come up in the writing. The entry that shows my realization is this one that I wrote in 2003:

'Looking back over this diary and earlier diaries, I realize that I keep making the same essential mistakes: looking outside myself for direction, always seeking approval from external situations, not enjoying the moment.' Geez, that took me long enough, didn't it?!

Now, I came to this after starting to do yoga that same year, to work on my back and neck pain, and after I just could not do any more pain-inducing exercises at the gym but wanted to stay fit.

My writing has been sporadic and dependent on external factors, but, hey, that is the way I usually am, so at least I am consistent.🙶🙶

Understanding what motivates you or drives your responses and desires helps you to understand the choice you are making (or avoiding making) and to live more consciously. Many of us remain quite ignorant of what drives us, yet that generally leaves us feeling as though we are living someone else's life rather than our own.

It's true that it is very easy to be self-deceiving when it comes to motivation. That's why it is often so much more useful to write—and keep on writing beyond the point of easy comfort—rather than simply accept the first bundle of thoughts that come to mind.

In the exercise that follows, I am suggesting that you further explore your motivation in journal writing, because that's where your focus is right now. But the same principles can be applied to almost any topic.

I am reluctant to paint the sitting room because...
I am refusing to speak to Alice because...
I never want to ask for anything unless...
I am keen to go on holiday with my old school friends because...
I am upset every time someone talks about how much money they are earning because...
I am eager to impress my boss because...
I find it very hard to speak up for myself because...
The reasons why I want to be a published writer are...

It's impossible for me to change my job (even though I hate it) because…
I can't tell my partner what I really think because…
Doing my best is essential when…

Your turn
☛ *"I am writing this journal because…"*

AS YOU START
Make yourself comfortable. Wherever you are, settle into the ease and spaciousness of your journal-writing mind.

Begin by noting the day and time as well as the place. ("I am sitting in the airport lounge waiting to fly to Tahiti. The plane's delayed but who cares…")

CONTINUE WITH
"I am writing this journal because…"

(You can also use this same exercise to explore any topic in the context of your motivation: "I am reluctant to speak up about my salary increase because…")

Each time you feel stuck, come back to your primary sentence, writing it out all over again, with whatever follows, until you feel the topic is thoroughly opened out.

If you feel "stuck" or distracted, write about that. ("I notice that I am finding it hard to stop worrying whether I am doing this right…" "I feel excited, like the time when I…" "I don't really care why I am writing this journal; all I know is that it feels like the right thing to do and I don't know how long it is since I did something this instinctively. Maybe the last time was…")

You will probably find that you first write about what's familiar, even a little boring. *Get that down.* Clear the space inside your mind. Keep going.

Whenever you slow down or feel stuck, just return to this same sentence: "I am…because…"

When your state of mind changes, write about that. ("I'm not feeling so strung out now even though I am finding it quite hard to stick with the topic, which does churn me up more than I would have thought…")

Write for at least twenty minutes.

No stopping to edit or rewrite.

END WITH

Complete this sentence: "My most compelling reason to write this journal seems to be…"

Don't reread immediately.

Let your thoughts "rest."

Your turn
➔ Walking, then writing

AS YOU START

Walk somewhere familiar. Take your journal and pen with you. Keep walking for at least twenty minutes. An hour's walking is ideal. Just observe, without criticizing yourself, how much of your walking time is spent in the present moment, observing your surroundings and taking them in, and how much time is spent far away from your body.

CONTINUE WITH

When you reach your outer destination, take at least fifteen minutes to write about the walk.

What did you notice that was new to you?

What did you notice that was familiar but fresh?

How was it to observe how "present" you were? What would allow you to be more present?

How did your body feel as you walked and made contact with earth, pavements, roads, and grass?

Describe something you saw in great detail, as though you were trying to make it vivid for someone who doesn't have your gift of sight.

Before you turn around and go home, spend a few minutes sitting and *just looking*.

GENERAL ENCOURAGEMENT

When you return home, or even in a day or two when you have more writing time, write about that walk and especially what you observed on the outside as well as on the inside.

Write also about *sitting and looking*.

Repeat this exercise often.

It's wonderful to keep doing it in response to the *same* walk, so that more and more you see the subtleties and details which are hard to perceive when the walk is new and more obviously stimulating.

END WITH

End your day's writing by completing this sentence: "What I observed today…"

Don't reread immediately.

Let your thoughts "rest."

CREATIVE JOURNAL WRITING

Liberate your curiosity

A mind that is stretched to a new idea never
returns to its original dimension.

—Oliver Wendell Holmes

There is in the British Museum an enormous mind.
Consider that Plato is there cheek by jowl with Aristotle;
and Shakespeare with Marlowe. This great mind is hoarded
beyond the power of any single mind to possess it.

—Virginia Woolf

Curiosity—the drive to know more than you do now—is one of
the ultimate gifts of human intelligence (along with a willingness
to have your mind or perspective changed). It makes inner growth
possible. It rescues you from boredom. It expands your world
beyond yourself. It demonstrates to you what an awesome and
infinitely fascinating universe you inhabit. It also makes you a
more interesting and perhaps even a more knowledgeable person.
And it is the essential oil for your creativity.

"We do not write in order to be understood," said Cecil Day-Lewis,
once British poet laureate, "we write in order to understand."

I believe curiosity keeps your mind supple as well as expanding
it, whereas "certainty" rigidifies it—and you.

Your curiosity will be enhanced in countless ways by journal
writing. But that's not all. Your journal is a great place to explore

your own attitude toward what it means to be curious. Many of us have a mixed response even to that rather loaded word *curious*. Crushing phrases resonate from people's childhood years: "Mind your own business." "Keep your nose out of other people's affairs." "Too nosy for your own good." "Curiosity killed the cat."

Yet genuine curiosity and interest are quite different from prying or superficial gossip. Curiosity drives high levels of intelligence and social engagement, and I suspect that at least some of the people whose company you enjoy most, who seem most alive and wide awake, are also likely to be unashamedly curious and interested in all kinds of ideas and people. They don't want to know just how things happen but why, and then what next? They want to dive into the richness of events; make sense of things; find and establish connections; go beyond what is superficial, banal, or familiar; enjoy it thoroughly when they are challenged by what is unfamiliar. There is room for doubt in their minds. They can also allow their minds to be changed as new information comes toward them and meets new insights arising within them. They don't want to decide everything in advance. And they especially don't want "everything" to be decided for them.

When I finally got around to thinking about changing the carpet in my house, long after the conversation with my sister that I recorded in my journal entry on page 8, the lively Englishman who came to my house to measure up turned out to be delightfully curious about the house, the people who live in it, my choice of colors, the paintings on my walls, and so on. But then he caught himself and began to apologize for his curiosity. At least until I told him that I am a writer and that curiosity is essential to what I do, and perhaps essential to what he does, too. "You must have visited thousands of houses," I said. "And have seen far further 'into' them than most people ever would. And surely every one of those houses tells a story about the people living in it?" "Absolutely," he confirmed. And then he told me that his interest in the houses he visits also gives him the confidence to make suggestions or to let people know when they are making a choice that is unlikely to be wise. I was left convinced that curiosity combined with warmth made him an exceptional salesman and a special person.

Writing in *A Book of One's Own* about perhaps the most famous diarist of all, the seventeenth-century Englishman Samuel Pepys, contemporary author Thomas Mallon says: "[Pepys] is blessed with a child's avidity for any new piece of entertainment, science, invention, fashion. He wants to know everything.... He'll discuss optics just after he's discussed teeth; go see an experiment in blood transfusion performed on a dog; marvel at a bearded lady; and wonder how this Italian sport of buggery he's heard about is actually performed.... He is what the next century would call a great booby. And his willingness to be one so freely is his genius."

Your turn
Valuing curiosity

AS YOU START
Think and write simultaneously.

Don't stop to plan, edit, or censor.

You may want to write complete sentences or just make brief notes. Either is fine. Experiment freely. Be curious!

Note the day and time of writing as well as some detail about the place. ("Monday. Jan. 16 Midafternoon. Everyone out. Sitting in red chair in Ann's old room. The air feels heavy. No sounds that need concern me.")

Make the entry personal to you. This is the only time when your own opinions and experiences are all that matter.

Be aware of what's going on in your body.

(As I wrote that familiar line, which I am repeating with more or less every set of instructions for you, into my mind came some old favorite lines from D. H. Lawrence's poem "The Snake." I am writing them down from memory because that's the way I would do it in my journal, and I am rushing to do this because they so wonderfully express the often-overlooked *physicality* of writing and writers: "A snake came up to my water hole / On a hot, hot day in June / And I, in my pyjamas for the heat / stood there and watched him.")

CONTINUE WITH

Are you, as you read this and as you prepare to write, in your pajamas for the heat? Or wearing a tea cozy for the cold? Are you in your best suit, ready to go to the office in half an hour? Has the baby been sick on your T-shirt once too often? Or are there cat hairs on your purple chair, as there are on mine? Have you kicked off your shoes? Are you rejoicing in the sun that is streaming through your window? Or glad of rain or the damp of a misty night? Do your bones ache a little today? Or are you blissfully sweaty, having just come home from squash and thrown yourself into a bit of hearty journal writing without a pause?

Love those details. Recognize them. Write about them. ("In autumn," wrote Lewis Carroll, "when the leaves are brown / Take pen and ink and write it down.")

GENERAL ENCOURAGEMENT

There are many prompts below. Take them slowly. Return to the same one as often as you want. Jump some and come back to them later.

You might spend several weeks on this exercise, moving very slowly through the prompts, getting "curiouser and curiouser" as you do so.

Time and outcome don't matter; only process. How lovely! (Or is it? Perhaps for you it is quite the opposite. Let yourself be curious about that.)

Take a minimum of twenty minutes to explore each time you sit down to write. The outer limit is up to you.

If, despite the prompts, you feel stuck, just return to the idea of "curiosity" and let it move you along. ("Funny that most of the people I admire for their curiosity or aliveness are long dead...")

TRY THIS

Explore the word *curious* from a number of directions (and ages and stages). Jot down all your immediate associations with it. Then perhaps your associations with those associations. (Think of these associations as stepping stones, allowing you to walk on water.)

When you see yourself as a child, do you see a curious child—and if so, curious about what?

Many children are taught to "mind their own business;" they are told, "Shut up and don't ask questions." Did that happen to you? Does that admonition linger? How do you want to change that pattern now?

Are there any stories or impressions that come to your mind when you savor the word *curious*? Are there people you regard as inspirationally curious? Have there been people who quenched or judged your curiosity?

Do you associate curiosity with any of the people you most admire?

Have you ever felt other people's curiosity was intrusive or "too much"?

What are the taboos for you when it comes to curiosity: "I can't go there!"

Look for what surprises you. Any associations, further thoughts?

Can you think of ways in which you can encourage and develop your curiosity, or would you rather call it "interest in life"?

Finish this sentence: "I need to know more about..."

Finish this sentence: "I wonder what would happen if..."

Finish this sentence: "I have never tried..."

Think about the people you know best. Now think about what *you don't know* about them. And are you afraid to ask?

Does your workplace afford you a range of experience and opinion? Can you be curious there? Is it intellectually stimulating? Or stultifying? What do you want to do about it? It is possible to make simple, repetitive tasks more interesting by focusing on them more closely rather than dividing your attention. That's the key to mindfulness and internal steadiness. Is this something you could experiment with in any area of your own life? (Let yourself be open here, since at first it may seem counterintuitive.)

I think of curiosity and aliveness as being twin qualities. Do you? What are the qualities you most closely associate with curiosity? What makes it even more powerful for you?

Begin a list of ways to develop your capacity for curiosity. It's a skill that can rapidly improve with practice. Journal writing will help.

This exercise is all about waking up your curiosity, so each time you repeat the exercise, finish by completing this sentence: "The most unexpected (or valuable) discovery I have made today is…"

Don't reread immediately.

Let your thoughts "rest."

Some practical suggestions

A routine for your journal writing supports what you are doing. It also keeps you on track. It isn't essential to write every day, but writing most days really does make a difference.

Sit somewhere to write that feels really good to you. Let go both physically and mentally before you begin to write.

Whenever you feel flat or "stuck," describe that state of mind in your journal. Be a scientific observer of your own condition. ("I kept writing in circles, just commenting on that, then suddenly I took off against all my own expectations…")

Go against the current tide that tells you "instant is best." That's only sometimes true in journal writing. Here you can be both tortoise and hare.

"Forget" what you wrote yesterday. Practice coming into this day freshly. Bring to your journal writing your capacity to be present in the present moment, even when you are writing about the past.

Are your expectations high enough? Do you feel like trying something more than you are at present? Taking greater risks with language or subject matter or point of view? Looking more attentively at what you might be avoiding?

Concentrating mostly on "thoughts"? If so, look at the feelings associated with whatever topic you are writing about. If you have written a lot about your feelings, take some time to review your thoughts. Or to be a little more analytical and detached than usual. Or look at these feelings themselves somewhat dispassionately. What do you *think* about those feelings? How precise are they? Are they your familiar repertoire? Could you think about your feelings with greater subtlety?

Notice with interest where you might be limiting yourself. What are you telling yourself that you can't afford to notice, feel, or write about?

Notice with interest what's exciting you about the journal-writing process. *Let yourself be surprised.*

Journal writing and you

I'm awfully scared that everyone who knows me as
I always am will discover that I have another side, a finer
and better side. I'm afraid they'll laugh at me, think
I'm ridiculous and sentimental, not take me seriously.

—Anne Frank

If I had to live my life again,
I'd make the same mistakes, only sooner.

—Tallulah Bankhead

At several points through this book I have emphasized that the relationship you will have to your journal writing will be unique to you. This is true of all art forms, and while your journal writing may not be "artistic" by any external measure, it is a direct reflection of you and your experiences.

It also changes constantly, like any other creative work or any other relationship. Different qualities are needed at different times to sustain it and get the most from it. I love the authenticity of that. It excites me that journal writing is *not* something predictable either in its content or in our attitude toward it. That is what makes it come fully to life for me.

Here's how Jo describes her journal-writing relationship.

Jo

❝For me, one of the challenges of the journey is 'discipline'—maybe it's being a generation X'er that I struggle with discipline. For while it is my belief that it is of great benefit to have a daily spiritual practice, followed by the journal writing, this requires discipline—making it a priority.

It's a bit like going to the gym and, like the gym, the more you use the muscles, the stronger they get. My 'emotional/spiritual' muscles are bulging at times, at other times needing a workout!

Both spiritual practice and journaling are easy when times are difficult—as they are like a lifeline—they help, they inspire me somehow to keep going. While they still help when things are good, they don't feel as 'essential' for survival—even though the insights and learning through this reflection process are powerful—they are easier to put aside, in favor of sleep-ins, morning news, snuggling children in bed, new love (!), etc. So I guess in a nutshell, for me it is about discipline. A deep inner knowing that it is 'worth it' when times are good, just to continue this 'knowing and exploration of self'.❞

The tone of Jennie's experiences is different. She writes like a painter. Your tone is likely to be different again. When you have read Jennie's experience, you might want to shut this book and without further prompting write a description of your journal-writing process so far. This time, limit yourself to a couple of paragraphs; go for intensity rather than length.

CREATIVE JOURNAL WRITING

Jennie

❝I find writing grounds me, makes sense of things in a way and invites movement within. It frees me up somehow. I find I move on. This just happens, it is not a conscious stoic thing of determination but rather a natural process. Like an inner sigh of thought. I have a simple wooden table with a fruit bowl, old jug, colored pencils and paints in a painted flowerpot, an ornamental bowl and an old broken bottle with thick glass full of lead pencils. I love this table. It quietens the room. My diary rests on this table in front of a wooden chair.❞

(Are you pausing to write right now? Do you want to create your own still life in words, *right now*? Or does a totally different aspect of journal writing engage your attention? Not right, not wrong; this is all about you and your inner world and the way you see things.)

An observant quality also comes through in the writing of Australian priest and author Edmund Campion, although *what* he observes is quite different from what Jennie has just described. These words are from *Lines of My Life*, a journal-based book that Campion wrote which was in part inspired by Thomas Merton, also a priest and an exceptionally famous journal and letter writer. (Merton is one of my journal-writing heroes, largely because of the quality of his observations and the depth of his considerations. Yet my own journals are almost entirely unlike his. Again, I want to emphasize that we can admire yet not feel any temptation to copy.)

Edmund Campion: Journal extract

I was asked to give a talk for Library Week…and I chose the topic "How Books Changed My Life." Sitting on buses and in waiting rooms, I jotted down random points as they occurred to me. Then, when I came to put the talk together, I found very few books in my notebook, even though I've been a reader all my life and the family used to say that I always slept with a book under my pillow to start the day. But influence? Changing my life? It would be hard to construct a convincing thesis from the few titles that had made it into my notebook.

Because Campion's champion (I have to take a moment here. That childish but satisfying wordplay "Campion's champion" is, for me, a very "journal-writing" way of writing that would never be permitted in the serious worlds of "writing for a living" or "getting published"). Let me start again, leaving the previous sentence incomplete. (Leaving sentences "dangling" is also deliciously "typical" of journal writing as is this overuse of brackets and quotation marks. The truth is, in your journal anything that pleases you *goes*.)

Campion's inspiration came from Thomas Merton. Here is a brief example of Merton's own journal writing. I picked it practically at random in order to avoid claiming it to be "typical." In the face of seven volumes of published journals, written over most of his adult life until his death in his fifties (in 1968), I would have to use the word *typical* with great care. These two tiny glimpses simply let you know that his vision of his journal was more than broad enough to encompass his intellectual (and his spiritual) life, while also offering him the place where he could anchor his visual, sensual, poetic awareness of the physical world and his place in it.

Thomas Merton: Journal extract

Today my usual routine was turned upside down—lately I have been intellectually overfed and in the mornings I read less and less. Today I read almost nothing at all in the early morning, a bit of Dorothy Emmett's book, which is good, and a couple of pages of the Castelli volume....

[Four days later] Strong wind and long storm of rain all day long, sometimes blowing up violently out of the south, bending the black pines and flooding my porch, sometimes dying off while rays of low cloud fly north under the iron ceiling.

And if, as you write, you long for your inner poet to get up and "speak," let me now show what you could do with a journal entry like Merton's—or your own:

From south to north

Strong wind.
Long storm.
Rain all day long.

Violence from the south.

Black pines bend, the porch floods.
Wind dying off sometimes.

Under the iron ceiling
rays of low cloud fly north.

This may not please your professor of poetry. If doing something similar goes some way to pleasing you, that's perfect.

Your turn
━● *Word juggling*

TRY THIS
Take a paragraph from your journal.
    Break up the lines.
    Move words around if that feels right.
    See how different they look and feel when they are placed in an unfamiliar relationship with one another.
    This is a chance not just to see your own words differently but also to play with words and surrender to their magic.

Faithful to the task

At fourteen, living in a modest house a long walk from the train station with my father, sister, stepmother, and two of my eventual four half brothers and sisters, missing my mother unbearably and also any sense of myself as a beloved daughter, longing to feel remotely confident despite my brashness, I instinctively recognized the value of journal writing. (I have a couple of earnest, typically embarrassing, deeply felt, totally unreadable journals that somehow survived all the moves from country to country and flat to house that characterized my adult life until my mid-thirties.) Nevertheless, I haven't always been faithful to journal writing myself.

Most years during my twenties and even into my thirties I read other women's journals avidly while simply not making the connection that I could be honoring my own story, too, and creating my own.

Even after I got back to journal writing—when my first child, Gabriel, was a baby and I was so totally enchanted with him I had to pin some of those fleeting moments to the page—there have been years on end when I felt that I was doing so much other writing professionally that to write "for myself" seemed impossible. I regret that.

The writing that I do in my journal is so different in so many ways from the writing I do professionally. I have demonstrated some of those differences here. And when I was again thinking about those differences and writing about them in my journal earlier today, it struck me yet again that my journal writing is far more intimate and domestic than my professional writing could ever be. And it's infinitely freer.

I write often in my journal about my children, friends and family, and our cats. In truth, what I repeatedly focus on is my everyday life within the house where I am much more mother and spiritual seeker than I am writer and spiritual teacher. This doesn't mean that I don't ever write about my domestic insights professionally; occasionally I do. Or that I don't explore my intellectual concerns in my journal; occasionally I do. And quite often I write about the *effects* of my writing life on me and the people around me.

My journal writing is, however, much less structured and guarded than when I am writing for publication. It's also often quite raw, and in the body of the writing I myself am more open, more heart- and less mind-driven.

There were periods of journal writing where I was writing faithfully and fluently, then suddenly stopped despite all kinds of events continuing to happen. I suspect I thought, "I will remember this. I don't need to write it down." Some of those times were the most joyous; others were the most harrowing. The sheer drama of those times should have made them unforgettable, but in fact each day brings new impressions and the old impressions—other than in broad outlines—get swept away. I don't regret having less detail about the harrowing times. In fact, I can't bear to reread anything I have written in those times, although I know that many journal writers do reread exactly those journals to see what they have learned and how far they have come.

It is the joyful times that I truly wish I had recorded more faithfully and in infinitely greater detail.

Here is another journal-writing story, this time from Lisa.

Lisa

66 My first journal cost me $75 more than 15 years ago and I was blessed to begin writing in it that very weekend with the help of an amazing writing teacher. Since that time I have had many journals, large and small, handmade and extravagant and $1.99 specials, but each have had their own lives, loves, and learnings.

In these books I have written out my hopes and fears, frustrations and fantasies. I have welcomed and farewelled love affairs, bemoaned the unending workload I faced at the time, and noted great books to read or films I wanted to see.

There have been days when I have felt so guilty about not writing, I have spoken to my journal, apologizing for my failings and promising to get back soon. Other days there is no solace or clarity until I can get my thoughts down on paper.

But the biggest blessing of all, the one that returns to me again and again, is the ability to look back on my life, warts and all. Going through these pages, I can begin to see patterns in my thinking and emotions, hear myself as other people might hear me, and watch the twists and turns of my mental meanderings.

I have learned much from my journal and cannot imagine myself without one. She is confessor, counselor, and caregiver, all rolled into one. 99

Some practical suggestions

🖊 **Experiment with writing more directly:** "Dear Journal…" Anne Frank addressed her journal (or perhaps her journal-writing self) as "Dear Kitty."

🖊 **Experiment with writing in the third person:** "Sam Brown has never done this kind of thing before…"

🖊 **Choose something you have written about in broad strokes.** Write about it now in much greater detail.

🖊 **Review how often you are writing "I think."** Switch to "I feel." Or vice versa.

🖊 **Ask yourself from time to time: What am I not looking at here?** Or "What am I *not* asking?"

Deepen your self-awareness

If you've heard this story before,
don't stop me, because I'd like to hear it again.

—Groucho Marx

We often feel enraged or insulted when someone misreads us or behaves toward us in ways that we believe are insensitive or outdated. Yet sometimes we ourselves are a little slow or reluctant to catch up with how we have developed or with what our current attitudes and interests really are.

Journal writing is a powerful way to stay in tune with your life right now. As Helen puts it, "Through my writing I have come to understand so much about myself & what I am feeling, as well as about the wider world…I often write to help me reintegrate."

This is in part because as you write you inevitably return to the center of your being, to your stable sense of "I." And also, when it comes to the art of reflecting, on which a sense of inner stability and self-possession depends, journal writing really is the "tool of tools."

Stretch and hold

Creative exercises can transform and support your journal writing.

They give you greater flexibility and skill as a journal writer.

They give you insights that you may not get through even the most sensitive recording of events.

They develop the details and originality of your own observations.

They affirm your creativity.

They push you to know more and to want to know more.

Keep recording events as often as you want.

Make time for creative exercises also.

Reflecting and ruminating

You may already be discovering what a tremendous difference there is between ruminating and reflecting. When you ruminate, you are likely to be turning the same fairly limited repertoire of thoughts over and over in your mind repeatedly. This may be fine. Sometimes those thoughts are comfortable or where you want to be. Sometimes, though—and especially if you are somewhat anxious or stressed—those thoughts are *not* lifting your spirits. In fact, they are confining you, and as the thoughts churn, you may even find that you are losing energy or vitality.

Reflecting is quite different. It is a powerful art that lets you look at your experience or your thoughts and make something of what you find. Reflecting requires some distance, but that distance can come *after* you have written things down. It may be only a tiny distance, even then, yet there is a sense still that you are looking at the situation, engaging with it rather than being overwhelmed by it.

It may also be that what you need to reflect on is a choice, especially when you feel at a crossroads regarding some aspect of your life. Or you may want to reflect on a particular relationship that is less rewarding than it might be. It could also be that you want to understand better your reactions to something or someone.

This doesn't mean writing and writing until you have insight. Insight does not want to be caught so directly. It has its own timetable, its own subtle ways of making itself known to you.

It is enough to clarify to yourself that you *want* insight and perhaps what you want insight about. Most or maybe all of our greatest insights arise from our unconscious minds if only we give ourselves the chance to receive those invaluable messages which sometimes come "wearing strange disguises."

My experience—and this has been confirmed for me by many of the journal writers I have taught—is that frequently asking the questions is far more potent than struggling for answers. As Nicky suggests, "My experience has shown me very clearly that we can get ourselves into a spin searching for the 'right' answers when what really gets us out of a hole is to be looking at the situation in a spirit of inquiry, opening our minds, not closing them!"

It's also consoling that the question does not need to be the "right one." If you remember that journal writing is more about process than outcome, this makes perfect sense. You may want to "ask the questions" over many days. Patience may be needed as well as tenacity.

The questions may change as the days pass. Trust that.

I love the following two quotes, which for me dramatically illustrate the power of asking questions, then leaving it to your unconscious to work them through.

We want the answers, when the questions themselves are more engaging....The question takes on new shades of meaning as we peel away the layers of ourselves.
—Ellen Sue Stern

Try to love the questions themselves, as if they were locked rooms or books written in a very foreign language.
—Rainer Maria Rilke

Troy describes his route toward understanding, which involves action and an engaged, trusting kind of waiting.

Troy

❝I am not a constant journal writer and I in fact only took it up because I had a long, incapacitating illness when I was thirty-one and was pretty desperate and my cousin, who happens to be a professional musician I wholeheartedly admire, told me that was how he had got through a bloody awful time himself. I thought it was quite upfront of him actually to tell me this so I started writing in a fairly hackneyed kind of way using the equivalent of school exercise books but because I had a lot of time then, I got into it more and more. I guess I taught myself to a large extent because I found out that I could write myself through a situation far more effectively than talking myself through it or boring someone else with it.

What I find is that once I have written something out I don't reflect on it all that consciously. In fact I prefer not to. What I do is that when I sort of feel like I want to write about that situation again, I simply go back to it, pick it up where I had left off, but of course I have actually moved a long way down the road.

I do use questions quite a bit. I have a special question book in which I am planting the 'seeds' of my questions then 'watering' those seeds with my trust. Even thinking like that is pretty much outside the box for me. I don't think I would have got to this point had I not originally been so desperate.

My journal writing is not all about reflection, of course, but reflection is the kind of secondary benefit that really is a primary benefit because I get so much from it. 99

For Carol, a journal is a "place of records" and journal writing is a way to "fill the gaps. Otherwise you would forget the details and the connections." You might notice in her entry below how the word *emerges* emerges twice, powerfully reflecting her inner processes.

Carol

66 My journal writing is the place of imagination, often linking my dreams and day-to-day reverie. These pages often culminate in some kind of prophetic message. Meaningful events stand out. A pattern emerges.

My journal also places me in the reality of writing out my anger, frustrations, and disappointments. I am eternally grateful my thoughts on these matters stay on the page, because in hindsight most incidents are on the learning curve. I don't fight them.

The more I think about my twenty years of writing in my journals, the more the events and their ripples stand out as a 'waking dream.' Dreams, a photograph, or a story from one of my design students somehow enmeshes my life. Purpose emerges. 99

It is so freeing to remember that journal writing is about process, not outcome. It is totally free of "productivity" demands. There is no right or wrong way to do it. There is just the doing. F. Scott Fitzgerald said it for many of us when he wrote: "All good writing is swimming under water and holding your breath."

Some practical suggestions

🖊 **Stretch your vision of what journal writing can be**—even when it feels a little strange. Strange can be good. Risk, at least sometimes, doing an exercise in a way that "isn't you": rushing when you might usually be very careful, holding back and repeating the same exercise when you usually value novelty.

🖊 **Hone your eye for detail.** This makes you look and think harder. It pushes you beyond the obvious. The smallest details may evoke the strongest memories or responses.

🖊 **Support your opening moments of journal writing.** Note the day and time, and describe where you are sitting to write as a way of taking yourself "in" to the reflective process.
  Note what emotions are already bubbling up.
  Be aware of what's going on in your body.

🖊 **Rediscover freshness.** Return often to the same prompt. Answer it as though you are reading the prompt and writing about it for the first time. Again and again, let yourself be surprised.

Your turn
● Love the questions

AS YOU START

Note the time and place of your writing.

Describe your sense of anticipation.

CONTINUE WITH

Discover: What question is in your mind?

Consider: What are you *not* asking? (This can be very usefully provocative.)

Once you have written your question down, give yourself time to reflect on it *as though you had never come to it before.*

You may want to begin by free-associating in words or notes rather than writing sentences.

GENERAL ENCOURAGEMENT

Let yourself write instinctively and freely.

If you find you are moving "off topic" or "off question" and writing about something else, *go with that.* ("My question was about getting in touch again with Joel, but soon I got to writing about how hard it is for me to know what I want for myself, how out of practice I am at standing up for what I want…")

Be aware of what's going on in your body and include that.

If you notice strong emotions or associations arising as you write, bring them into your writing.

If the same or a similar question arises over days, weeks, or even months, then honor that. Keep coming back to it freshly.

END WITH

Finish by completing this sentence: "Today I learned…"

Also write: "And I still want to ask…"

Don't edit, criticize, or rewrite.

Let your questions "rest."

Where home is

What you know in your head will not sustain you in moments of crisis.... Confidence comes from body, awareness, knowing what you feel in the moment.

—Marion Woodman

Absence of home, the being cut loose, creates a kind of freedom. Like adolescents escaping from the parental abode, we become able to test our new identities, to find other selves lurking within. Yet without discovering home, I suspect we are unable to truly grow up. Home implies not just rest and ease, but work and commitment.

—Kathryn Heyman

Home and *self* are two of the most powerful words in any language.

You can explore the idea of home as a way of understanding yourself better. You can also let yourself find out more about what the idea of home means to other people.

Be aware that *home* is a very potent word. We live in a world where many suffer homelessness or have experienced great pain in their homes. Go slowly if you know there are painful associations for you. Don't force anything.

Teasing out the layers of this topic, you may want to draw, sketch, or paint rather than write. That's also part of journal creation, and it can give you tremendous insights and sometimes a very surprising experience of release. If you are routinely thinking verbally, drawing can be especially helpful. It absolutely does not matter if you are good at drawing or hopeless at it. The idea is to think in images and get those down.

Free drawing

"Free drawing" follows the same principles as free writing.

~ Allow yourself to choose colors as well as images quite instinctively.

~ Keep going. Don't stop to analyze.

~ If one drawing leads to another in a free-associating kind of way, follow the trail.

~ When you have finished the drawing or drawings, let them "rest." Don't try to decide what they mean there and then.

~ You may want to finish by writing about how you feel, what emotions came up, what surprised you. If you are writing after drawing, keep your commentary to observations of the *process* only. ("It's years since I have drawn anything, and it was only the sight of those thick, lustrous, waxy crayons that seems to have got me started. I am shocked but quite thrilled too that I have filled several pages and time really did stop—in fact, I sat back only when I realized that it had got rather dark and cold. More than an hour had slipped away, but time was filled with these great rosy colors.")

CREATIVE JOURNAL WRITING

Your turn
☛ *Exploring "home"*

AS YOU START

Make yourself comfortable.

Note the time, date, and place of your writing. Because you are going to be writing about home, make this more detailed than usual.

Focus on where you are today and how your room looks to you. Write in detail about the chair you are sitting on, the walls, the little table in the corner that used to be in your friend Alex's house, the way the light falls on your collection of shells…

More briefly, describe your inner state as you begin to write. ("I feel like I should be doing my tax return so that's a bit of a familiar struggle between duty and desire.")

CONTINUE WITH

You may want to start simply by writing all your associations with the word and idea and experiences of *home*.

If you notice strong emotions or associations arising as you write, include them in your writing. ("It's funny, but as I write about home I am feeling really frustrated with myself that I don't invite people here more often—that somehow I've got out of the way of…" "I remember making sets of cushions when I was first married. Fat cushions stuffed with hope.")

Choose from the list of prompts below. Return to the same prompt as often as you want.

GENERAL ENCOURAGEMENT

Keep writing for at least twenty minutes without stopping.

Push through your boredom by including your observations of that in your writing. ("I seem to be back writing about my horrible job yet again…so maybe it is time to do something about it, but today I had thought I was writing about home so why is it that I can never feel 'at home' in any workplace when I give work all that time and attention?")

Choose one prompt only at a time. Let yourself go into it deeply.
Give yourself time to reflect on it before writing.
Once you begin, let yourself write instinctively and freely.
No stopping to edit or rewrite.
Be aware of what's going on in your body.

When I think of the word *home,* I…
"Making a home" is something that…
My first home was…
For me *home* means…
What I value most about my current home is…
I feel as though I am missing…
My ideal home is…
What makes a feeling of home for me is…
I feel "at home" when…
When I think about home, I remember…
The smells of home for me are…
People matter more to me than place…
The most important room for me in any house is…
I could only write this journal at home because…
For me home is not a place at all…

My idea of "home" changed when...
The objects in my current home I'd rescue first are...
The idea of "home" for me extends way beyond four walls...

END WITH

At the end of your writing, note if there have been any shifts in the way you think about home—or yourself.

Finish by completing this sentence: "What struck me most today is..."

MORE ENCOURAGEMENT

Whenever you return to this powerful topic, try to set aside what you have already thought and written.

Don't forget that in addition to drawing, you can write poetry, add photos, or gather up postcards of paintings that show exteriors or interiors of homes.

What you are searching for is atmosphere primarily, and the associations and resonances of meaning that come with it.

Your turn
☞ More on "home"

TRY THIS

Ask a few people close to you about their idea of home. Write not just about what they tell you but also about your *responses* to what they describe. (Your responses are more useful here than their opinions.)

Find a piece of writing that expresses "home" for you. Or a piece of music. Or make a special dish or recipe that conjures up home. Write about that experience.

What does your home "need"? Write about that. (Who says so? Is it what you think it needs or what would look good?)

Let your home write a letter to you. ("Dear Isabel, I love the way you put on such haunting music whenever you dust me...")

Explore what you feel about the world's homeless. Then explore what action feels right to you—if any.

Take some photographs of your home, visual snapshots that you can then write about, including what motivated you to photograph and write about "this" rather than "that."

Discover how far your sense of "home" extends: garden? apartment building? street? neighborhood? country?

Make a list of quotes about "home." Here are some that I love.

Opening the window, I open myself.
—Natalya Gorbanevskaya

Home is the place where, when you have to go there
They have to take you in.
—Robert Frost

Home is where the heart is.
—Anonymous

This is my city, the hills and harbour water
I call home.
—Lauris Edmond

Swimming at a depth of thirty meters,
I once entered a cave through a low, narrow opening....
It was there I found my God.
—Enzo Maiorca

A house does not need a wife
any more than it does a husband.
—Charlotte Perkins Gilman

For many journal writers, the journal itself is a mini home. Rosi calls her journal a *haven*, a word that for me powerfully expresses "home."

Rosi

❝I first began scribbling in a notebook eight years ago when my marriage was beginning to unravel. I needed to set things down, to have an outlet for the emotions to tumble onto the clear white pages, to keep my own record of this awful and often painful trajectory, with the tiny hope that one day it might become simply a memory.

I had bought a notebook in Venice, on a trip to Italy. Its cover was of marbled green with swirls of ochre and cream. Each page was decorated with a tiny frieze of famous palazzos or grand mansions. The notebook became a haven. It recorded the raw emotions that surfaced, the challenges I faced, moments of happiness and hilarity, and the old companions of shame and loneliness that dogged me for so long.

I wrote in it almost every day for five years.

Recently I read it from cover to cover. And I was astonished by the amazing wisdom that was revealed in page after page.

I realized that I had understood so much more than I could ever have imagined about what I was experiencing and why. (The separation had unleashed a wave of unexpected anger and resentment from my ex.)

Initially I was full of wonder. Later I was despairing about how I seemed to have been unable to translate that knowing into action.

But that little book is now so full of wisdom and knowledge that it has become a talisman, reflecting for me that we have the solutions within to so many of the problems we confront in life...if only?

Somehow we need to be more able to use what we write, to help us to make more sense, and to be the observers of our own wonderful lives.

Anyway, the good thing I guess is that it was all there for me. Maybe I just wasn't ready before this?❞❞

In this tiny extract from *Gift from the Sea*, a book that for me has the intimacy and honesty of journal writing, Anne Morrow Lindbergh captures the complexity of what "home" can mean to many of us.

The life I have chosen as a wife and mother [of five children] entrains a whole caravan of complications....It involves not only the butcher, the baker, the candlestickmaker but countless other experts to keep my modern house with its modern "simplifications" (electricity, plumbing, refrigerator, gas stove, oil burner, dishwasher, radios, car, and numerous other labor-saving devices) functioning properly. It involves health....It involves education....It involves clothes....It involves friends...and endless arrangements to get together.

In my novel, *Tasting Salt*, I wrote about the home of my central character, Cordelia, in such intense detail that many readers sent me letters saying they had experienced the house almost like a character itself. The interesting thing is that I chose to make the houses in the novel places without a particular national context. I wanted the universal feeling of "home" to exist regardless of whether it was Melbourne, Montreal, or Madrid that I was "seeing" as I wrote and that readers were experiencing as they read.

Here seventy-year-old Cordelia is being speculated about by Laurie, a much younger friend. The tone is very different from the Morrow Lindbergh extract above, but that journal-writing intimacy continues. What is also clear here is the way that "home" and people run together somehow, that in observing one we are often saying a great deal about the other.

Who indeed knew what went on in the private recesses of Cordelia's life? The social floors of their tall, narrow house are the two lower ones. These are largely occupied by their gorgeous big kitchen and a rarely used formal dining room on the ground floor and a sitting room on the first floor that manages to be spacious and intimate at the same time. Spacious because it is a big, traditionally shaped room with long, formal windows at either end. Intimate because it is so colorfully decorated: walls, curtains, cushions complementing—but in no formal way *matching*—furniture, paintings, lamps, *objets*—including big and little statues from the East, India I suppose, though maybe Indonesia and Thailand, too—that are invariably stunning and personal— even sometimes quite quirky. They could only have been chosen with love. There are a couple of bathrooms, too: one big, one little. Also colorful; dashing, even. It's intrigued me to notice that Cordelia decorates them with lavish vases of fresh flowers that are often more copious than those used in the more obvious rooms for flower arrangements.

But for all that space and detail, there are still two more floors above those "public" floors, and they have come to seem to me to represent in some unfathomable way what you simply cannot know or pry into with Cordelia. Parts of her mind are like that, too: shut off from public viewing. One can almost see a little gold rope going across, and a discreet notice warning off trespassers.

It is impossible to leave the topic of home behind without sharing a few lines from May Sarton, a poet and novelist and one of the most loved and read of all published journal writers. The lingering, highly detailed, and sometimes very practical details of home and garden fill her published journals and have delighted her readers for decades. This glimpse of her work is from *Journal of a Solitude*, perhaps the very best of her many volumes. It was originally published in 1973. I mention this date because what it means to "keep house"—and especially to decorate—may have become more and not less inhibiting. Yet the world of creative journal writing thrives on color, detail, texture, contrasts, contradictions, and depth!

May Sarton: Journal extract

Standards of house-keeping and house-decorating have become pretentious and competitive....When I was writing a column for *Family Circle* I had planned one in praise of shabbiness. A house that does not have one worn comfy chair in it is soulless. It all comes back to the fact that we are not asked to be perfect, only human.

What a relief it is to walk into a human house!…That means not so much efficiency as life enhancement: a cat sitting on a table to look out, a bowl of flowering bulbs, books scattered about.

Here is a last example of home reflections, this time from my own journals. Once again, you will notice how one thing leads to another…and another.

Stephanie Dowrick: Journal extract

In my meditation chair. 6:30 a.m. Cats fed. House quiet. Rain.

Feel safe. It's almost seven years since I moved into this house, and only now would I say it is completely home and I have given up regretting A. Street [my previous house]. I do regret selling A. Street still, but this house is now thoroughly wrapped around me—or I, it. No. It's the parcel, and I am in it. What made the difference? Such little things: painting it in colors of my own choosing, getting rid of the carpet I hated, opening out some of the rooms more by getting different furniture or rearranging furniture. And I also think that there are more elemental changes that go on when we enter a house and then live in it for some time. Does the house pick up our vibrations? Our smell? Does it resonate to our hopes and dreams? Surely it must. That has to be what we mean by "atmosphere" rather than aesthetics. I am aware now that it would be extremely hard for me to leave this house, yet I am also keenly and unpleasantly mindful that as I get older leaving this or any other house will be inevitable. And not for a while but eventually forever. Sometimes I look around and think how would it be if I never saw this again, would I feel the tug…leaving? And how would it be for my children and loved ones to see the house…but not me in it? This doesn't feel morbid; it is the other side of love. I love life so much and am so hugely grateful that I have this house in which to live that life.

If I were to live another 30 years in this house that would be wonderful. (Living 30 more years would already be a blessing. I long for that.) Would I be any more reconciled to leaving it then? I doubt it. Perhaps eventually my knees would give way although to date my knees are loyal friends. And when the children are no longer part of the house and the cats have gone, what differences would that make? But even when they are not here there will be echoes of them and maybe that is what these seven years have already given me: layers.

When I think about Gran's house and garden in Feilding I think of literal *layers*. I see piles of books, read and unread. And lots of letters, written and received. But no pens? Surely never biros? I don't recall fountain pens, but there must have been. Too many photos and ornaments. Clothes shed, shoes kicked off. I have too many photos too—although what does "too many" mean?! They are all treasures. Gran had so many tiny ornaments in glass-fronted cabinets, relics of the traveling adventures to Europe that meant so much to her. She probably spent three or four years traveling and ten times that number of years passionately recalling her adventures, which were probably extremely tough at the time but high gloss in the remembering.

Remembering the cabinets, I am kneeling down in front of those glass doors again, a long-legged skinny girl peering in, begging to be enchanted. We were easily enchanted. No television. Only books. As many books as we wanted from the little side-street Feilding library. No world travels. Just stories of the rest of the world, brought back home to be told and retold. I hated hearing most of them. I liked the ornaments much better.

Tiny things telling us where we have been. Tiny signs telling us where we might be going.

Another side of journal writing: sign reading.

Rain heavy now but soundless.

A source of freedom

Writing a journal is a way of honoring your own life, taking it seriously even as you open to the energy and spaciousness that creativity brings. Writing a journal also brings invaluable freedoms.

Freedom to know your own mind(s), conscious and unconscious.

Freedom to choose your values and to live them out.

Freedom to see what drives you.

In the West we generally take the idea of "freedom" as a given. Yet how can we treasure it fully if we don't truly understand what freedoms matter to us and why? It's wonderful to explore this topic not from an abstract point of view, as in "Freedom is a good thing," but from discovering how it is embedded and lived out in your everyday life. Where do you have choices, and where do you believe you do not?

Xanthe's experience echoes that of many journal writers: that writing a journal, and maintaining some constancy with it, frees you to engage with life more intensely even as you "get back to your center" as Xanthe expresses it. That is my experience also.

Xanthe

❝What I get out of my journal writing is so much. I am able to reread entries and see how things have shifted for me in a period of time, whatever that may be. For I know it is easy to forget some of the color of emotions that the experience may have had for me with the passage of time. It also keeps *me in touch with me*, for the act of setting aside the time to write means I get back to my center, without all the outside noise.

Also, having been journal writing for over 20 years, it has created the wonderful habit of being observant of how I move through life, what impact things have on me, being observant of the signs that I notice along the way that make this journey so much more joyous and myself more present. It most definitely is a part of my spiritual experience!!❞❞

Your turn
●❯ *How free?*

AS YOU START
Make yourself physically comfortable.

Note the date and time. Describe where you are sitting and how you are feeling.

Choose one or several of the questions below as your focus. Or ignore the questions and go straight to your own thoughts and feelings about yourself and freedom.

CONTINUE WITH
You are writing about freedom, but make it personal, not abstract. Looking at any topic in direct relation to your own life and concerns will immediately make it far more meaningful than if it floats as a word only.

First, simply use the word *freedom* to free-associate.

Invite a string of words to jump from your mind onto the page. ("Free to understand myself…no one coming into my room without knocking…including the 'rooms' of my mind…KEEP OUT…")

Don't stop until you have made a satisfying number of jumps.

NOW TRY THIS

Did you envisage that adult life would "set you free"? And has it?

Whom do you know whom you think of as "free"?

In what areas of your life do you feel free to be yourself?

How will journal writing increase your sense of inner freedom and choice?

How does your ideal of freedom fit with getting along with other people and making allowances for them?

Have you given yourself permission (freedom) to love your own life and enjoy living it?

GENERAL ENCOURAGEMENT

Keep writing for at least twenty minutes. If you give up too soon, you will quite correctly believe you have nothing to discover.

Don't stop to edit or rewrite.

Notice what is happening in your body. Write about that.

Don't feel that what you write has to be "worth your while" or especially meaningful. Judging yourself in that way gets in the way of writing freely.

"My most valuable discovery today is…"
    Don't reread immediately.
    Treasure your discoveries.

Naomi writes about how her journal writing was a key support in finding the essential freedom to meet a difficult situation well—at least some of the time.

Naomi

❝Persistence—was that the key, you ask?

I was so disoriented by sadness and by whirling, anxious thoughts that at its worst I was quite delusional. All the same, at core I am a hopeful person, and eventually my functional, practical self began demanding that I find ways to 'earth' myself.

Mostly instinctively, but also through conscious determination, I chose a range of physical disciplines that worked for me.

Firstly, there was writing my journal, absolutely religiously, no matter how much I didn't feel like it.

Secondly, I walked 4 kms every day, without fail, with my two dogs.

Selling my business, I took a job as a chef in a Buddhist teaching institute (which all my associates thought beneath me) and began two of the most important years of my life, leading directly to where I am today. The period in the Buddhist kitchen (which I ran single-handedly and which was equipped to meet the dreams of any chef) was one of intense reconstruction. Cooking is such sensate work, engaging all your senses and really taking you out of yourself if you let it—and the best part is that at the end you bring simple pleasure to people and you see it in their faces.

During that time I had the closest thing to an epiphany. One day, lost in the meditative rhythm of chopping and peeling, the thought emerged, completely unbidden, that my life didn't matter at all. Not in a negative sense, but via a glimpse of the continuum, in comparison to which my little earthly life was quite irrelevant. What a relief! In the next instant I realized I was free to do, to live, to think, to be exactly as I pleased."

The exercise that follows offers you another chance to learn more about yourself and about freedom. Circling a big topic, looking at it from a number of directions, and coming back to it repeatedly as the sun rises and the moon sets is part of journal writing. Everything does not have to be new in order to be fresh.

It's also so good to remember that you don't need to write anything "important" just because this is an important topic. Start and finish "where you are." You are writing for self-discovery, not to make a point.

Your turn
❧ A bouquet of freedoms

AS YOU START
Note the date, time, and place of your writing.

Note your state of mind right now. ("Wondering if I have anything to say…")

How does your body feel right now?

Take a few moments to reflect on which of the freedoms listed below are most important to you.

Freedom to know your own mind(s), conscious and unconscious.

Freedom to choose your values and to live them out.

Freedom to see what drives you.

Freedom to know what supports you.

Freedom to be creative (in your own way).

Freedom to understand yourself as well as others.

Freedom to make good use of your own insights.

Freedom to understand what really matters to you.

Freedom to make mistakes. (How else can you learn?)

Freedom to stop repeating your mistakes!

Freedom to discover what you need to do about challenging situations.

Freedom to live at the center of your own life while becoming less self-centered.

Freedom to observe your own life unfolding.

Freedom to care about the lives of others.

Freedom to behave well.

Freedom to extend your creativity to every corner of your life.

Now choose just one "freedom" to write about. (You can come back to the others.)

As you begin, be sure to note down the thoughts that arise with your choice. ("Most of all I want to find out why Mum said we could choose our own careers but then...")

GENERAL ENCOURAGEMENT

Keep in mind the freedom that you have chosen. If you had more of that particular freedom, what would that give you? How would your life be different? Would the way you see yourself or others—or the purpose and meaning of your life—change?

This is a topic that you may want to return to a number of times. It's fine to go back to the same "freedom" many times.

Notice if there are any "freedoms" you are consistently overlooking. Risk writing about them.

Write for at least twenty minutes.

END WITH

Finish by completing this sentence: "The most precious gift this freedom gives me is…"

Don't reread immediately.

Let your thoughts "rest."

That was how it felt to me

The cracked crab that I recall having for lunch the day my father came home from Detroit in 1945 must certainly be embroidery....I was ten years old and would not now remember the cracked crab....Yet it is precisely that fictitious crab that makes me see the afternoon all over again.... That was how it felt to me.

—Joan Didion, *Slouching Towards Bethlehem*

Writing the facts

Your life in your journal

For many journal writers, recording the facts *is* journal writing.

Hilary

❝I have been keeping a journal for 20 years. It started as a form of therapy while I was recovering from a long illness, and I just kept going. I write every day, the highlights and lowlights of my day. I tend to write mainly about events. There's not much about my feelings or thoughts. It only takes me a few minutes, quick and easy. I guess that's how I can write every day because it doesn't take long and doesn't require much effort. Sometimes my diary entry is just a few lines, rarely more than a page. I write in exercise books and have filled 68. I can't *not* write each day. It's as necessary to me as water or food. No matter how awful I'm feeling or how busy I am, I'll still write in my diary. Occasionally I do forget, but I'll remedy the oversight the following day.

I often wonder, why do I do this, what does this compulsion say about me? I once read a short piece in *The Age* about someone who had died and left 30 years' worth of journals behind, they even published some extracts, and I thought, 'I'm going to do that.'

It still shocks me to reread the entry I made on the day my husband died. It is so unemotional and matter of fact, just a bald account of the circumstances of his death. Thinking about this now, perhaps it's not very surprising because I was just following my routine patterns. Perhaps also in writing my diary as usual that night I was trying to get some semblance of normality back into that terrible life-changing day.

Also, for the past five years [since her husband died] I have kept a separate journal in exercise books which reside in the drawer by my bed. These notebooks number nine so far. I use them to work through problems and painful feelings and the general emotional 'baggage' of life. I just write in these books now and again as the need arises. It's not so compulsive! I find the process immensely satisfying, helpful, and a huge release.❞❞

As a creative journal writer, you are always free to go beyond the mere recording of facts. ("Went to Newcastle. Saw Tom.") Facts can be a useful prompt for later writing or reflecting and on those days when you have barely had the time to comb your hair or floss your teeth, then perhaps a few "facts" may be all that you can manage. But more usually, regard the facts as your well-sprung diving board and the world of impressions, ideas, and reflections as the bottomless pool into which you can, at any time, fearlessly dive.

In one of the essays about journal writing that I most value, "On Keeping a Notebook," which is part of her altogether tremendous book *Slouching Towards Bethlehem* and absolutely worth seeking out, American writer Joan Didion explains that for her the point of keeping a notebook (a journal) was never to have a "factual record" of her thoughts and events. What she is interested in is *"How it felt to me."* And often that is evoked by apparently minor details that may or may not be strictly factual but exist in ways that transcend fact. She is talking in her essay about the kind of journal writing that I am describing throughout this book, not for public consumption but something private, intense, playful, relieving, and unashamedly subjective.

My hunch is that many people get discouraged writing their journal when it is too "fact focused." Leaving all the facts out would also be a tremendous pity—a disaster! Those "facts" are the details of your life. The secret is to bring to the facts your writer's mind: curious, open, lateral, creative, vulnerable.

The process of "fact transformation" is, at the very least, twofold: a commitment to detail and reflection on the facts. Add to this the issue of discernment: *Which facts?* After all, if you constantly write about how unfair everyone is at your workplace, without gaining any insight and without looking at least sometimes at what else is going on in your life, eventually (or quite soon) you will bore yourself. If you never write about your passions, you will bore yourself. If you only write what you think other people would approve of (should they find your journal and read it), you will bore yourself. If you write to deceive yourself, to whine or endlessly self-justify, you will most certainly bore yourself.

If, however, you let your mind, your imagination, your instincts *roam*, you will never be bored. I can guarantee it. Recognizing that you are *always* choosing what you will notice and pay attention to, and *taking charge of those choices*, is one of countless benefits of journal writing.

The creative exercises in this book are all developing the skills needed to find the details that will mark your writing as *yours*, that will stretch you to reflect in ways that are satisfying, that will allow you quite naturally to "roam" intellectually and emotionally, finding your way toward what is fulfilling and avoiding what is not.

These skills will transform your "facts" writing. They will keep it fresh. They will make it more personal. They will certainly make it more insightful—and that word *satisfying* comes to mind again. Journal writing can be intensely satisfying even while it remains, like the life that it mirrors and records, truly a work in progress. (As journal writer Carol says: "The journal stores the angst, the connections, and the mystery.")

Venting

Most journal writers *vent*, at least sometimes. For most of them this means expressing and releasing strong feelings without worrying much about whether they are fair or justified. Self-justification may even be part of venting for many journal writers. The intensely subjective outpourings of "venting" can bring relief. They can also bring insight.

Venting can be used also to "rehearse" a difficult situation: writing in the journal what you feel, then facing the actual situation with greater equanimity and peace of mind. (The examples below emphasize that.)

It's also a version of venting that happens when someone writes a letter within the pages of their journal *that will never be sent*. This may be to someone who is alive and has hurt you; it may be to someone who is long dead. The actual proximity or availability of the person is irrelevant; writing such a letter, and releasing the emotions within the safe place of your own pages, can be tremendously powerful. It can also enable you to move on and pay attention to more encouraging and uplifting aspects of your life.

My hunch is that venting can be outstandingly useful, one of the most powerful emotional benefits of journal writing. What I would hasten to add, however, is that "venting" is rarely enough. It is like using a very limited number of musical notes or the same two or three chords constantly. It is likely to be most helpful when it is part of journal writing and not all of it.

Here are some remarks from journal writers about venting in their creative journal-writing practice.

Carol

66 My journal also places me in the reality of writing out my anger, frustrations, and disappointments. I am eternally grateful my thoughts on these matters stay on the page, because in hindsight most incidents are on the learning curve. I don't fight them. 99

Neil

66 I actually went to an anger-management course in my late 20s and was instructed to write out my feelings. I didn't keep a journal in those days and in fact would have regarded it as ridiculous and girly. If I hadn't been more or less obliged to do this I wouldn't have had the guts because, frankly, writing things out in black and white you can't help but see them differently and sometimes the whole self-pity house of cards comes tumbling down somewhat. I also wrote out some of my full-on grief feelings. That wasn't venting in the fast and explosive meaning of that word. It was very slow. In fact, I would say a line or two was hard to get down. But I could then say, 'That's me, too.' And I did feel much better. 99

Venting raises privacy issues rather fast. You may not feel that you can write or vent freely if there is any chance that your words will be read by other people. Sometimes it is worth considering venting on loose sheets of paper that you can keep in your journal and will destroy when you feel ready. It may even feel extremely satisfying to destroy those pages, perhaps with some feeling of ritual as you burn them or tear them into tiny pieces with a conscious sense: "This is over."

Jo has decided that she will let even her darkest pages "be." But this is a personal decision for every journal writer. Once again, there is no right way, just your way. Jo also says that she writes more when life is difficult than when things are going well. I suspect that is true for many others also, although as I have already noted in this book, my personal regret about journal writing is *not* writing more during those good times, not treasuring those details and making them available in years to come to my older self.

Jo

66My journal writing began in earnest when my marriage ended. This event was an unexpected and shocking shattering of my 'world.' Struggling with excruciating grief, and at times only continuing for my young daughters, I used my journal as therapy. Every morning upon rising I sit, coffee in hand and journal. Mostly handwriting in my 'diary'; at other times tapping furiously at the keys on my computer.

Journaling became a sacred space for my thoughts. I recorded my nightly dreams, spiritual insights, hopes, fears, pain, goals, and experiences—documenting my grief, my learning, my journey.

Eventually it also included all the things I thought everyone else was sick and tired of hearing about—the 'stuff' I just couldn't say to anyone else any more but for whatever reason still needed to 'say.'

I reread my journal often and am surprised at times at how far I have come, at other times, laughing at the repetitive nature of my writing. Same old issues! Lessons still to be learned.

My journal in some ways for me is like my own personal 'cheerleading squad,' where my writing winds around from expressing my emotions (usually pain and grief) and then winding my way back to peace.

I made a decision for my journal writing to be raw and real and unedited and only for me. I have decided to 'trust' that others will respect my privacy. I have even thought about my children reading my journals (even when I die)…and have decided to just 'let it be.' It has been nearly four years of daily journaling for me, and I have occasionally written 'This is more a record of my pain and grief than my true existence.'

I do this because this is the reality for me. When things are at their toughest for me, I write. It gives me solace. When I am soaring, sailing along, I write less. It is then that I know, in writing this, that, yes, perhaps someday my children will read my journal, and they will know my innermost deepest thoughts. Perhaps they will learn from my journey, and if that's the case, the 'exposure' is worth it.❞

Venting is generally part of journal writing rather than the whole picture. Terri expresses this, capturing the "seasons" of journal writing that will be familiar to many.

Terri

❝As a child I kept a diary of happy events. As a teenager it became more of a 'secret confession.' Skip ahead 20 years and one marriage, a brother's suicide, two daughters, and one divorce, and it provided a sporadic outlet for my loneliness. Five years later it sizzled with the excitement of new love, new hopes, and new dreams. A few years on, the savage bite from the 'black dog' 20 years previously festered, and my diary entries bled with disappointment, bleak unhappiness, and negativity. Its sole purpose was to 'contain' my depression. Two years ago I sought help, and my cloud has lifted.

My new journal is a celebration of my rebirth. It radiates hope, enlightenment, and love.❞

Venting is a form of free writing. It is usually highly instinctive. It may feel "driven." The goal while venting is almost always just to get things out. Reflection or insight may come as you are writing. If that happens, it is worth including right then and there. ("Now I can see that…") Often, though, you will simply feel the need to empty out all the thoughts that have accumulated or built up, along with the feelings that the thoughts arouse. When you have done this and feel emptied, in a good way, or released, reflections or insight often follow, although sometimes not immediately. It helps to have fewer rather than more expectations.

It is worth reminding yourself regularly that while we often choose what we will write about instinctively or consciously, as we write, our unconscious mind can quickly take over so that we find ourselves writing about something else altogether. This is characteristic of venting, and it is also the gift of free writing and free associating. Tapping into your less conscious mind is one of the greatest possible gifts of journal writing. It takes you beneath the surface so fast to the deepest reaches of your existence.

Start and finish with the details

It is fatal not to write the thing one wants to write at the moment of wanting to write it.

—Virginia Woolf

Let's go back to Newcastle and Tom. ("Went to Newcastle and saw Tom.") This could have a great deal of meaning for you, but does writing it in this way offer much satisfaction? You may remember Tom and that day perfectly as you write those six words, but years from now, this description will remain one-dimensional. You are absent from it. What you felt is absent. And, other than those couple of facts, the day is also absent.

It's always the details that arise from your own observations that make your writing your own. Journal writing is where you can be flamboyantly, outrageously subjective. This means paying attention to:

- ～ The physical details of time and place
- ～ Your emotional and sensual responses
- ～ Your analysis—if that seems relevant
- ～ Your impressions and observations (or your "hunches": "It seems to me that…")

Impressions may quite naturally include your emotional responses and are often more important than the events themselves. "Went to Newcastle fairly reluctantly. Sense of duty probably. But when I saw Tom it was really clear to me how much he had been looking forward to this visit, and my initial embarrassment that maybe I was pushing myself forward somehow just dissolved. I was really sorry that some kind of stubbornness made me dress that morning in one of my most hideous jumpers, but I really think that…"

In *Writing Down the Bones*, writing teacher Natalie Goldberg fine-tunes the details wonderfully of a highly subjective viewpoint and account. "Be awake to the details around you, but don't be self-conscious. 'Okay. I'm at a wedding. The bride has on blue. The groom is wearing a red carnation. They are serving chopped liver on doilies.' Relax, enjoy the wedding, be present with an open heart. You will naturally take in your environment, and later, sitting at your desk, you will be able to recall just how it was dancing with the bride's redheaded mother, seeing the bit of red lipstick smeared on her front tooth when she smiled, and smelling her perfume mixed with perspiration."

And it so easily could have been: "Went to the wedding. Danced with the bride's mother." Or just: "Wedding."

Your turn
━◆ Adding details to the facts

AS YOU START

Quite spontaneously choose a single incident that you experienced within the last couple of days. (Keep it to something that is still fresh in your mind.)

Write down a description of that in *fewer* than ten words.

Now give yourself some minutes of quiet reflection and begin to recall the details of what you experienced.

Start writing again, describing the same experience in *at least* 300 words. (You choose your goal without imposing an outer limit!)

As you "scan" the event, review it from "afar" and close up.

Finish this sentence: "The detail that brings this day most to life for me is…"

I would suggest that you repeat this exercise often. It is also a great one to come back to when you recognize that your journal writing is falling a little flat.

The purpose of the next exercise is simply pleasure, pleasure in words and your own impressions. It will also show you how marvelously plastic language is: how you can bend it into all kinds of shapes and see something different each time. I will use Natalie Goldberg's writing above as an example. Once again, this may not please your poetry professor, but when it comes to you and your journal writing, she, along with the judge and critic, can be safely and permanently retired. Kick up your writing heels!

Bride in blue
marries groom
with red carnation.
Chopped liver on doilies.
Bride's mother smiles and dances.

Your turn
━● Water into wine

TRY THIS

Take two or three details from any situation in your journal and look closely at the words you have used to describe them. Then take them out of context and play with them.

You can simply scatter them, and perhaps you will notice in a way that you didn't earlier how many colors you have described, or what foods or which smells, or what emotions keep returning to ask for your attention.

Write about what you can now see that you didn't see earlier.

Or you can move those same words around until they resemble, in their short lines and intensity of expression, a "poem" like the one above, which I hardly want to call a poem, as even that feels like a restriction.

Use your physical senses

Lovely night, warm, and filled with gentle summer
noises. I don't feel like writing.... Instead I am
going to listen to the whispering trees.

—Edda Walker

The details of a situation will always come into your mind with far
greater clarity when you tune into them via your physical senses:
seeing, hearing, tasting, touching, feeling, thinking.

How did your body feel as you sat through the meeting?
What was it like to be touched (physically or emotionally) at the
gathering after the baby's christening? What was the physical
environment like when you went to inquire about the new job?
What were your feelings as you went up the stairs to the building?
What kind of environment would you name as "ideal"? Do you
know what you are looking for or want? How did the place smell?
Did it "feel" safe and friendly? What was the person's quality of
voice? How did you react to that? (Do you know how your own
voice sounds to others?)

Recording these details does far more than enliven your journal
writing; it trains you to observe even the most unpromising
situations with far greater interest and subtlety. Waiting for a
friend, for example, on a busy city corner could be an experience of
total frustration. ("Where is she? How dare she be late?") Equally,
it could be an exercise in observation: of the people rushing by

you, the heat from the road, the loneliness of someone sitting at the bus stop opposite, the crazy number of fast-food outlets, the absence of organic markets...

It could also be an invaluable exercise in self-awareness. ("I felt really impatient and upset first off. Then I decided to forget Celeste entirely and just notice that if I relaxed my body and especially my knees a bit my mind could also go down into first gear, and I could chill completely without much effort. So it was actually a bit of a jolt when she arrived, totally flustered because her bus had broken down.")

It's all in the details (and attitude).

Your turn
➤ The power of your senses

AS YOU START

In greater detail than usual, describe where you are sitting, the time of day, the atmosphere inside and outside, how your body is today. Go for precision, not broad strokes. Check all your senses.

CONTINUE WITH

Describe a situation that happened several years ago. Pick something instinctively. Run it through your mind like a movie. When you begin to write, for the first ten minutes or so, focus on what you *think* about the situation. As you continue to write, switch your focus to your *feelings*.

Then, after another ten minutes, switch again, emphasizing thought over feelings. You may want to comment on that switch as you write.

As you are writing, look down through the tunnel of time and bring each moment into even greater color through the power of your senses.

Remind yourself what the place looked like, what the atmosphere was, how it smelled. How did your body feel? Who else was involved? What challenged, pleased, or surprised you?

END WITH

Finish by completing this sentence: "The sense I now have about this situation is…"

And then: "The sense memories that seem strongest for me are…"

Let yourself also notice any differences between observations driven by thought and those driven by feelings.

Don't reread immediately.

Let your thoughts "rest."

The next exercise shows how much can be learned or gained when your focus becomes intense. The rose—or the object of your attention—becomes your trainer and your meditation teacher, settling and strengthening your mind.

Your turn
☛ Observing the rose

AS YOU START

Place a single rose where you can easily see it.

(It need not be a rose. It could be any other flower. It could be the head of a cabbage that has gone gaily to seed! But simply sit, looking at your gift from nature.)

Allow yourself to merge with it, and when your thoughts wander, come back to it again.

Write in detail about the rose.

Describe it to that unfortunate being who has never seen, touched, or smelled a rose and has no idea what you are talking about. Push yourself to notice the details you usually rush by.

Finally, write in detail about how it was to be simply present, in the presence of something so ordinary and so wondrous.

Write also about how it felt to have your attention so focused in this form of meditation.

Relax into a few more minutes of quiet meditation with your rose.

Not doing, *being*.

Reflections and impressions

I think these difficult times have helped me to understand better than before how infinitely rich and beautiful life is in every way and that so many things that one goes around worrying about are of no importance whatsoever.

—Isak Dinesen

Reflecting on the "facts" and recording your impressions of the "facts" is at the heart of writing creatively in your journal.

On November 5, 1936, the great English writer Virginia Woolf, having just finished her novel *The Years*, wrote these lines in her journal (published in *A Writer's Diary*): "The miracle is accomplished. L. [her husband, Leonard] put down the last sheet about 12 last night; and could not speak. He was in tears. He says it is 'a most remarkable book'—he likes it better than *The Waves*—and has not a spark of doubt that it must be published. I, as a witness, not only to his emotion but to his absorption, for he read on and on, can't doubt his opinion. What about my own? Anyhow the moment of relief was divine. I hardly know yet if I'm on my heels or head, so amazing is the reversal since Tuesday morning. I have never had such an experience before."

As your own familiarity with creative journal writing grows, you will quite naturally develop the capacity to go beyond the facts.

Journal writing itself will teach you to:

~ Value and create detail
~ Identify emotions/drives/desires/satisfactions
~ Look beneath the surface of events
~ Check your senses
~ Observe yourself somewhat dispassionately
~ Look at events and interactions from other people's points of view
~ Discover the emotions that are driving different situations
~ Find the patterns in your own emotional habits and reactions—and in your observations.

Almost all the exercises in this book, plus your own processes of journal writing, will very naturally increase your capacity to reflect fruitfully. It is also possible to take almost *any* situation and look at it from the perspective of your own inner Wise Being or Higher Self.

Value your discoveries

Intensify your capacity to reflect. At the end of each day's writing, ask yourself: "What did I discover today?"

Take your time with this and if possible repeat it more than once: "What else did I discover? And what else?"

This question may refer to your day or to your journal writing.

Allow yourself to be surprised.

Write down your answers.

Your turn
Reflecting skillfully

Let yourself choose just one of these options.

You can write a letter to yourself from the perspective of your Wise Being or your Inner Wisdom. ("From my perspective, it is fairly easy to see that what was being argued about was not whether Paul should have been allowed to go to camp but how you and James both feel about making decisions on the run, especially when the pressures seem...")

You can also write an account of a complex situation *to* your Wise Being.

Finally, you can write out a question to your Wise Being and leave it in the safety of your journal, coming back to it only when you feel ready to write the answer.

CONTINUE WITH

Take any situation you have already written about in your usual way, and look at it from this higher (deeper?) perspective.

Keep refocusing so that your perspective remains broad, positive, and compassionate.

You may need to be patient. Sometimes you will need to return to this exercise more than once.

Remember, you may also want to write *to* your Wise Self rather than *from* your Wise Self, setting out in detail what is of concern to you.

Keep writing for at least twenty minutes.

Complete just one of these sentences:

"The insight I most value is…"

"The action I need to take is…" (Perhaps you will see that no action is needed.)

"I am most grateful to see that…"

"I feel more hopeful now because…"

Don't reread immediately.

Let your thoughts "rest."

Yourself and other people

Writing in your journal gives you a chance to go back over your day and extract meaning from a hurried meeting with a friend or retrieve the significance of some fleeting event.

—Janette Rainwater

Much of your "factual writing"—facts, feelings, impressions, opinions, inner commentary—will involve other people. This mélange will express your thoughts and feelings about how they experience you and how you experience them. What you choose to focus on, the feelings it expresses, the points of view it opens out or hardens, will also tell you a great deal about yourself.

In *Slouching Towards Bethlehem,* Joan Didion writes this (I love the raw honesty of this comment!): "I imagine...that the notebook [journal] is about other people. But of course it is not. I have no real business with what one stranger said to another at the hatcheck counter in Pavillon....Nor is my concern with a woman in a dirty crepe-de-Chine wrapper in a Wilmington bar. My stake is always, of course, in the unmentioned girl in the plaid silk dress. *Remember what it was to be me*: that is always the point."

The topics that follow in the next exercise may be all that you need through many weeks or even months of journal writing. And that's terrific! Continuing to circle the same topic opens up all kinds of subtleties. Whichever topic you choose, it will support you to write about yourself and others—and about yourself *through how you think about others.* (This will not make you more self-centered; on the contrary, as you come to see how often your own projections color what you write, you will gain more clarity and a greater sense of choice.)

Your turn
✏ *Other people and you*

AS YOU START

Focus on *this moment.* Note the day and time, and describe where you are sitting to write and also something about how you feel right now about your physical environment.

Note what emotions are already bubbling up.

Be aware of what's going on in your body.

Tune in to all your senses. "Scan" the situation from the perspective of your senses.

CONTINUE WITH

Choose one or two topics from the list below. Push yourself for more detail than is readily available. Keep going back to the same prompt or question.

Note what your inner commentary is as you write about these topics. Include those inner thoughts.

Think about the last time you met someone new. What did you think of them? What did you tell yourself about what they thought of you?

What would you like someone new to notice about you?

What's likely to interest you most about other people? What drives your judgments?

What makes it easy for you to be "yourself" with others?

What would it mean to accept someone at face value?

What allows you to feel accepted and at ease?

Which of your qualities is most available for others to appreciate? Do you make it easy for others to understand and like you? Is there anything you would do differently if…?

Is it comfortable for you to look at events from a perspective that isn't your own? How do you feel about practicing that right now, writing a persuasive description of a situation from the point of view of someone else? Choose a recent event if possible.

Think of someone close to you. Write a description of their state of mind right at this moment.

When you got dressed today, what did you want your clothes to say?

If someone was looking at you as you sat on a park bench or at a bus stop, what "story" might they tell themselves about you? Could you write that story now?

GENERAL ENCOURAGEMENT

Whichever topic you choose, write for at least twenty minutes.

Don't edit or rewrite.

Don't judge or criticize.

If your "free-associating" takes over and pulls you off topic, know this is fine! It is always worth following the trail of your own thoughts. It can be fun to look at how one thought prompted another.

Return soon to this exercise and pick another topic until you have covered them all (especially those you are most reluctant to tackle).

Complete this sentence: "It was fascinating to discover that…"

"I now see that ____ is more complex/understandable/ likable than I thought because…"

Let your thoughts "rest."

Meeting someone new

Regularly record in your journal your impressions of new people and new situations. This will help you hone your instincts, especially when you recognize how wrong you can occasionally be!

It may be enough to write a quick snapshot of someone, but do note the qualities you believe they have (or lack). And then keep your eyes and ears open.

Also check whether you are routinely looking for ways to take a genuine interest in other people; that lifts your own spirits.

Shifting viewpoint

It is often possible to shift your perspective most usefully by describing a complex or emotionally loaded event from someone else's point of view. ("When I wrote about our fight from Kate's point of view it made me much less tense….I knew I was fighting about nothing much.")

It can also be helpful to look at a difficult situation from the perspective of someone you regard as a flexible and creative thinker.

And occasionally, it can be a nice version of venting if you exaggerate your *stuck* point of view in order to get to the other side of it and beyond.

Your turn
➤ Another viewpoint needed?

AS YOU START

Choose a situation that you have described one way in your journal, then put yourself in the place of others who are closely involved and try "seeing it" from their perspective.

It can be helpful to "hear" their voices and language as you write.

Get into character as fully as you can.

Think about their attitudes in general as well as in this situation.

CONTINUE WITH

You may eventually want to "answer back" in your own voice. That's fine, but do so at another time. This time, give the "alternative" point of view a real chance to be heard.

Write for at least twenty minutes.

Don't stop to edit or rewrite.

If you notice strong emotions or associations arising as you write, include them in your writing.

END WITH

At the end of your writing, complete this sentence: "It is so refreshing to discover…"

Don't reread immediately.

Let your thoughts "rest."

Ask "How has my mood changed since I began to write today?"

There may be noticeable changes. At other times the change will be subtle. Either way is just fine.

You may also want to ask "Has my thinking changed?" or "Do I now see my day differently?"

Note that also.

Some practical suggestions

Notice which events consistently invite your attention. Notice what is consistently left out. Are you choosing? (How come you are always writing about the people who cause you grief but never those who support or delight you?)

Date your journal entries. Also note the time of day you are writing. You may be surprised how differently you see things midday as opposed to late at night. A few lines or even a few words about where you are, physically, can often get you started and make you more satisfyingly observant.

Note the circumstances of where and when you are writing. ("Taking precious time between meetings...") *Before* you launch into a description of the meeting that went terribly wrong or wonderfully well, ask yourself, "How am I now, right at this minute?" Record your answer. ("Tonight I feel exhausted but agitated." "Today I feel rather slow and dreamy.")

Add flesh to the bones. You may be in a rush to get down some bare facts, but even then give yourself permission to add some color and detail. Ask yourself: "What's engaging me here? What's interesting me? What's happening beneath the surface of things?" Observe the difference between recording an event and an impression of that event. Notice that impressions can be passionate and dispassionate.

Be yourself

Truth is such a rare thing, it is delightful to tell it.

—Emily Dickinson

Your details, what you see and seek, intensify the creativity of your journal writing. They wake you up to see the world in more vivid color. They widen your vision and excite your senses.

Honing your insights and instincts, and setting down your thoughts on the page, you will feel more balanced and grounded in your everyday life. You will feel more entitled to your opinions but much less defensive of them. You will be able to take knocks and disappointments more easily. (And gain insights from them.) You will be able to appreciate the good moments with increased ease and trust. You will have more to think about. Without even trying, you may feel more alive.

I discuss reviewing the process of journal writing a little further on in this book, but I do want to say here that in my experience rereading is part of being "yourself," understanding yourself more confidently, and tracking your own unique journey. Rereading the exercises (and how you felt about doing them) can be as fruitful as recalling memories through rereading the "facts." Many of the journal writers I have quoted here refer to that directly or indirectly. Here is what Veronica experienced.

Veronica

66 The guided practice of retrieving my journal 'hand' [through doing guided creative journal-writing exercises] was so rejuvenating for my spirit. It was like rediscovering an old friend and sharing all the stories I'd been waiting to tell them. Finding the space to reconnect with my writing is a treasured gift and I gained many insights through the regular practice—recurring themes revealed, low ebbs documented, and moments of joy all captured.

Sometimes, rereading something I'd written a day, a week ago jolted my senses with its stark contrast to my current state. Did I write that?

My first Living Journal is long finished, and while it was with great sadness that I put 'her' aside for those rocking-chair days to come, I have continued the practice of journal writing and, in that, the unending journey of self-discovery. 99

Writing out of town

We sit on a wall in the shadow of El Caracol, sensing the presence of long-dead spirits. We say nothing to each other for almost an hour....My heart beats fast, from the pressure of awe and from the more immediate fear that we will be caught by the Mexican guards.

—Doris Grumbach, *Extra Innings*

A number of the journal writers who tell their stories in this book were hurtled into journal writing during a tough time. Or sometimes a tough time—and wanting to write their way through it—intensified their journal-writing practice. It has also been true for me that I have turned to journal writing more faithfully when I have needed the particular mix of clarity, relief, and even comfort that journal writing brings.

A gentler but also powerful impetus to write your journal also often arises when you are out of your routine, traveling on business or on holiday, especially when you are experiencing a great deal inwardly and outwardly and are prepared to record it.

Keeping a journal while you travel means that you bring those rapidly changing experiences home with you, not only to your physical home but also to your inner "home," your storehouse of invaluable memories.

Rereading even a few lines will take you back to where you have been: to sights, sounds, smells, and, most of all, to *how it felt*.

It will intensify the experiences as you read them, and bring the memory of that time vividly into the present, where you are. Here is an example of the weave of observation and reflection, self and place, that is characteristic of "out of town" writing, this time from my daughter's journal.

Kezia Dowrick: Journal extract

Fiji has turned out to be a really fantastic holiday destination. Sean surprised me with the holiday. And what a surprise it's turning out to be. Today we went on a jet ski safari. I had to really confront my fears about the ocean and going fast on a jet ski, let alone 20 km off shore. I must admit I was very scared. It is strange cause I am such a confident swimmer but once again have had to realize that I am quite scared of boats and the ocean.

It felt comfortable riding on the back of the jet ski with Sean as he's grown up jetting around the harbor. He was very excited. I was excited too but so fearful at the same time. I told myself if something went wrong I would have a life jacket, and I would be with Sean. We have always said to each other that together we could do anything and try anything. So I told myself that this was the perfect adventure to share with him. That helped a lot.

The jet skiing was a little frightening, but once we got going it was just spectacular. We flew on the warm pristine waters of Fiji, through the Mamanuca Islands. We stopped on an isolated sandbank to snorkel. Saw beautiful coral reefs and brightly colored fish, then jet-skied around some more islands that really belonged on a postcard: white sand and aqua-blue water.

When we came back to the resort I felt proud of myself, proud that I pushed my limits and especially proud that I went out of my comfort zone. And I was really pleased that I could share the moment of achievement with Sean.

Am writing this sitting out on our balcony overlooking the beach. It's still warm even though the sun is going down. Sean is reading. A long, wonderful day.

The physicality and emotional range of experience of those few paragraphs capture an intensity and authenticity that is beyond a camera's range. *It's still warm even though the sun is going down.*

Here is another word painting that, again, offers more texture than a visual image alone ever could. Here, too, it is the details and the sensual impressions as well as the quick rift of emotions that make it so satisfyingly vivid for the writer to record, and also for us to read, glimpsing it over the journal writer's shoulder.

Subhana Barzaghi: Journal extract

There is no other place on earth quite like Mother India. The outstretched hand and the bottomless need of millions are unavoidable here. The poverty-stricken face of India is always confronting and challenging, no matter how many times I visit. Each visit manages to be a blessed thorn in the heart that niggles away at my conscience, a sharp reminder of the privileges and comforts we have in the West. As I encounter the harsh and exotic life of India, I practice keeping my heart and mind open in the face of such poverty, filth, overpopulation, hardship, and suffering.

Just outside the hotel, David and I stepped into an auto-rickshaw, and she stepped out of the morning fog. Tattered sari, baby on her hips, brown hand outstretched, clearly signaling in sign language: money for food. Our eyes met, hers pleading for a second, then a pervasive blankness, perhaps a protection against the inevitable disappointment of rejection and never having enough of even the basics of life. I do not avert my gaze, yet a part of me so easily could just look away, close my eyes, close my heart, and not even bother to give this poor soul a second thought. Mother and child, symbolic of Mother India and the millions and millions of poor families that stand behind her in the shadows, that live in the mud villages, that squat in the slums that cling to the cities' edges.

She extends her hand, I feel her desperation and plight. I put my hand on my heart and send her love, but I feel as helpless as her. I have no change left, I have already given handsome donations to the Dailets living in Bodh Gaya. I simply cannot give to every beggar; there are 82 million people in the state of Bihar alone, one of the poorest states in India, perhaps on this globe. Our rickshaw takes off, hurtling down San Sang Marg, her brown empty hand, her tired eyes leave a stain on my heart.

I want to use this journal extract to show you, again, how you can play with your own words and images, and create something different from the journal writing itself, exploring your own creativity, enjoying what words can do, creating bridges between yourself and your imagination. The words and images I have chosen are those that jumped out at me. They are not the "right" words; nor are they necessarily the most "important" ones. In fact, because the choosing is itself totally subjective, the writer herself may have chosen differently.

Sitting in the auto-rickshaw, we see
the woman standing.
Tattered sari, hand outstretched.
82 million people needing.
My purse is empty.
Her hand too.
Tired eyes stain my heart.

Your turn
🖊 A way with words

TRY THIS

Take a paragraph or two from your journal. The subject matter isn't important. It will be easier if you choose something that has some strong images, however.

Now scatter the words; write them out separately on a page or even on small pieces of paper that you can rearrange in a number of ways, and see how you can sew just a few of them together again, making something new and different.

Accessing memories

The journal itself will become a treasure-house of your memories. In the creation of it, however, you will also elicit more memories, deeper and truer than is possible through reminiscing or conversation.

Photos, books, movies, stories from friends and family, old journals—these can all prompt memories. So can the exercises in this book and the continuing processes of journal writing itself.

Creating a treasure

Wrap your journal in a beautiful cloth.

Treat it like the treasure it is becoming.

Take time to enjoy the ritual of unwrapping and wrapping, of beginning and ending your day's writing.

When you are accessing memories, it helps to go back into that time, writing from that perspective in the present tense. ("Mum and Dad are out at one of their endless church functions. I am reading in my room even though it is almost too hot to breathe.…Henry and Mark are playing cricket outside. They will look like beetroots when they come in for tea. I wish we had a pool like Jennifer's family: big pool, cool house. I want to be able to swim, but I hate going to the public pool when…")

Whether you are accessing memories from the past or writing about today, it takes courage to write honestly and to look somewhat dispassionately at what you write. Short-story and journal writer Katherine Mansfield urged, "Risk! Risk anything! Care no more for the opinions of others, for those voices. Do the hardest thing on earth for you. Act for yourself. Face the truth."

It takes even greater courage to allow yourself to be changed by what you find, to be genuinely affected, not just to see the world and yourself differently but also to act and respond more thoughtfully. It takes courage. Yet nothing else is worthwhile. Writing with honesty and in pursuit of honesty deepens your self-possession. It not only stabilizes you inwardly but also enables you to know yourself in the depth of your being, perhaps even at the level of soul.

A quotation that constantly inspires me is from Bengal poet Rabindranath Tagore (called "the Great Sentinel" by Gandhi). Tagore said, "Our true life lies at great depth within us." Writing faithfully, with courage and honesty, allows us to discover and live that truth. In the description that follows, Robbie shares something remarkably similar, discovered from her own journal-writing experience.

Robbie

❝You know how when you sit still and quiet and stop all that 'busy-bouncy' sort of inner dialogue and you come to that still, calm place? It feels like being completely 'centered,' calm yet flowing, unscattered. Centered. Subtle though it is, you can really tell the difference between centered and uncentered writing. The one brings with it a lightness, an expansion of heart as well as mind, a kind of 'serene aliveness.' And the other? I don't quite know how best to explain this feeling, but it's as if it 'wet-blankets' your vibration…covers it in treacle and muffles that vibrant serenity.❞

Your turn
⚷ Accessing memories

Writing is not the only way to access memories. Sometimes it is good to prompt memories in other ways and then write about them. Here are some suggestions. You will have others.

You could cook an entire meal that you remember from your childhood. (Wonderful to do this with friends or siblings close to your age.)

You could play some "hits" from when you were younger and recall what you were doing and feeling when that music meant most to you.

You could reread some of the books you most loved in different decades of your life or look at movies from key times.

You could trade stories with someone from the past who was important to you.

You could use your own body as a prompt. When did you get the scar above your left eyebrow? What was the year you finished growing? When did you start coloring your hair? At what age—if ever—did you feel "grown up"? When did you become aware of yourself as a distinct and unique person?

You could describe in detail to a friend (of more or less the same age as yourself) what your passions were in each decade of your life. And then listen as your friend describes their own memory journey.

You could look at photographs, and then write in detail about what was happening before and after the frozen moment in which the photograph was taken.

You could draw, drift, dream, allowing your mind to free-associate. Then, when your mind lands on something you believe is fruitful, you could pick up your pen again and return to writing.

Questions of choice

It's hard to think back in a journal, so much happens each
day. That week in the Midwest already seems far off. But
what remains vivid now is the memory of the plains…and
on the last day a visit to Ethel Seybold's ancient farm.…
She and her sister work at it as if it were a poem.

—May Sarton

What you choose to write about will determine the insights you
are gathering up for yourself. It will also affect your pleasure in
journal writing. This doesn't mean that you should only write
about what is uplifting. On the contrary, the question is far more
about whether you are limiting yourself or expanding your sense
of possibility: "moving through a pathless land."

Writing instinctively, you may feel that your subject matter
is choosing you. That's at least partly true, in my experience. It
doesn't mean, though, that you are not also choosing. (After so
many years not writing about my work in much detail, and writing
about my home life in a lot of detail, I can see, for example, that
at some level I have actually chosen *not* to write in my journals
about the inner workings of my books. Or what it means to me
to be a writer. I do write about the practical struggles of making
time to write and the effect on me and on my family of successive
projects. But that also feels personal. Other professional writers
have made very different choices.)

Consciously choosing engages your will as well as your mind and heart. It brings you into the center of your own existence where you can feel in charge. Consciously choosing also means that you are becoming a more skilled observer of your own life. Again, this doesn't invite cold detachment. It does support a greater sense of inner stability, openness, and freedom. I am drawn to the way these two writers express a similar thought.

> I have one outstanding trait in my character....I can watch myself and my actions, just like an outsider.
>
> —Anne Frank

> I want, by understanding myself, to understand others.
>
> —Katherine Mansfield

Before you explore the issue of choosing what you most want to write about in your journal (and whether and how you are choosing), I would urge you to explore the issue of choice itself. The question of choice will be a constant thread through your journal-writing life, mirroring your life as whole. Teasing out this topic consciously is of real benefit.

Your turn
⬤━ Circling choice

AS YOU START

Note the date, time, and place of your writing. ("At my desk. A quiet moment, remarkably.")

Note how you are feeling right now.

Choose to add more details than usual (or choose not to!).

Check if your first reactions to this topic are familiar or even a bit stale?

Now free-associate, writing down a string of words and ideas about choice without pausing, judging, or censoring.

Choose one or more of the following topics. Keep your writing personal and subjective, not abstract. Where you can, write about a particular situation that will keep your insights relevant to your daily life.

What does the idea of "choice" mean to you in your personal, emotional, professional, and family lives?

Do you ever say or believe that other people are "choosing" for you?

Do you usually exercise choice consciously, aware that you are choosing and not driven by habit?

Do you let circumstances "choose" for you?

Are your moods and emotions a matter of choice?

Are your attitudes, values, beliefs, a matter of choice?

Is the way you act and behave in line with your choosing?

Do you see how your life as it is today has reflected moments of choice? Were most of those choices consciously made?

Is what you write about in your journal driven by choice or habit?

If you could choose to shift your life slightly, what differences would that involve and make?

Note what has most surprised you.

The next exercise is also about choice, but in effect what I am suggesting here is very much what you will do quite unconsciously each time you pick up your pen, open your journal, and begin to write without a particular plan or exercise guiding you. Every time, you are choosing.

Your turn
●━< *Greater choice*

TRY THIS

Each day presents you with many things you could write about. But your mind flies to one topic rather than another. ("Here I am, worrying again about whether Rod is doing all right in London.")

This time, *consciously choose*. ("I won't write about Rod today. The issue of whether or not I stay in this job is really what I want to pay attention to, even though I absolutely hate thinking about it.")

Start with: "Today I am choosing to write about…"

Be ready to take off in another direction at any time. ("I thought I was choosing to write about my fears of getting old, and suddenly I was writing about my darling friend Caroline.")

If you do change direction, notice that you are choosing to do this and also include some commentary on that choice in your writing.

Write for at least twenty minutes.

No stopping to edit or rewrite.

END WITH

Complete this sentence: "Choosing this topic I have discovered (or experienced) that…"

Don't reread immediately.

Let your thoughts "rest."

Reviewing the process

I have just re-read my year's diary and am much struck by the rapid haphazard gallop at which it swings along…if I stopped and took thought, it would never be written at all.

—Virginia Woolf

There will be times when quite instinctively you feel you want to read rather than write. And how wonderful it is to be able to look into your own life through the pages of your journal. My suggestion is that you read *receptively*, mirroring the writing process, rather than critically or judgmentally. At the same time you may want to allow yourself to observe, while you read, the details of what you are discovering, not least about yourself and where the emphasis of your concerns lies.

Patricia speaks for many of us when she says, "Rereading my journal reminds me to be a bit more patient with myself as I deal with the past and try to move on with life. I find it very useful."

From time to time, when you are in a comfortable, expansive frame of mind, read back over your journal writing. Do this *not* to criticize it or look for ways to improve what you are doing but to discover more about the processes of your inner world and state of mind and feelings, and more about the processes of journal writing itself.

At times you will reread purely for interest. Sometimes you will reread because you want to recall events, access memories, see how far you have come, or better understand patterns in your life. No matter what your reason for rereading, when you have been writing for some time you will amaze yourself with how much you have forgotten even when some events felt deeply imprinted on your mind.

I like Janine's sense of adventure, choosing to reread journals at random.

Janine

❝I never let myself reread something unless it is several months old. My favorite thing is to choose a time of year and look back through my journals to read what I was doing, say, around the time of my birthday, or the anniversary of my mother's death, for several years in a row. Sometimes I just choose an old journal at random and read for half an hour or so. I definitely have a much greater sense of continuity with my own life than I could imagine having if I didn't write a journal. I feel like my life definitely belongs to me and to no one else. That's a good feeling on the whole.❞

Annie has been journal writing since childhood, but it is her travel diaries that she rereads with most pleasure.

Annie

❝I started writing in a pretty diary ever since I was about 10. Even at that age I needed the diary to look a certain way; it had to appeal to me.

As a creative child, expression and observation seemed to come quite naturally to me, and when I was observing keenly what was going on around me, I remember feeling a need to collect my observations and experiences in one way or another. I still have one of my unfinished diaries, and now at 44 I still occasionally write about certain experiences.

When I travel I take a journal with me. At the start of my travels I observe, experience, and collect data. Then I feel my experiences, and then I draw, photograph, and write.

On arrival back home I revisit my journal. I may remember new things which I add on, extend. As time goes by I look through and feel my experiences all over again. It makes me happy."

Marion uses her journal writing and her rereading of it to help her "get sorted as a writer." "Everything I wish to write goes through the journal first, and is reread, before going further. I am writing articles and also a history of my family. I find my journal is my close friend."

If you feel you want more depth or insight from the process of rereading, or you have questions about how you could be writing, then the following exercise will prompt you to read with special interest. Don't burden yourself with too many questions at once, however. Just pick a couple at a time, depending on what your own needs are.

Your emphasis in this multilayered exercise is on reading rather than writing. Nevertheless, you may want to have your pen handy and your journal open to note any impressions, observations, or ideas that arise as you read.

Your turn
✒ Reading your life

The daily journal is like a mirror. When we first look into
it, the blank pages stare back with ominous emptiness.
But if we keep looking…gradually we begin to
see the face that is looking back at us.

—Marion Woodman

The following questions are prompts only. Just choose one
or two to hold in your mind as you read.

They should not make you critical of what you are reading.
My intention is to encourage and remind you what journal
writing can give you.

AS YOU START

Make yourself very comfortable.

Turn off your phone.

Allow yourself a big smile of satisfaction that you have
something to read: all your own work. Bravo!

CONTINUE WITH

Hold just some of these questions very lightly in your mind.

Are you focusing on one area of your life only?

Are you writing about positive events as well as painful
ones?

What emotions or attitudes is your journal writing
enhancing?

Are you allowing your journal writing to develop your
sense of what's good for you and your life?

What talents or interests in your life is your journal writing supporting?

Are there relationships or connections in your life that need more enthusiasm or interest?

Are there any relationships or connections in your life that need more distance? Have you been writing about that?

Are you anchoring your insights by writing them down?

Are you celebrating joys? And writing about them?

You inevitably influence and affect other people. How is that reflected in your pages?

Are you letting the world outside yourself come into your journal?

Are you taking time to notice what is fruitful and rewarding?

What are you risking?

What are you not yet risking?

GENERAL ENCOURAGEMENT

Reading may be enough. If you want to be more active in your reflections, these additional questions may be useful.

How happy are you with the amount of time that you are giving to your journal writing?

Think back to your original motivation for keeping a journal. Bring that up to date. It will tell a fascinating story.

If your journal writing has been halfhearted, write about that. What does it tell you? Be curious rather than self-critical.

END WITH

Finish this sentence: "Congratulations to me for…"

Spiritual writing

To live in the world without belonging to the world summarises the essence of the spiritual life. The spiritual life keeps us aware that our true house is not the house of fear…but the house of love, where God resides.

—Henri Nouwen, *Eternal Seasons*

Spiritual genius is the uniquely human ability to seek life's meaning. It's the voice inside us that keeps asking What's it all about? Who am I? How can I make a difference?

—Winifred Gallagher, *Spiritual Genius*

Contemporary American writer Thomas Moore has suggested that exploring your spiritual life through writing in your journal "is not just a way to communicate or keep a record; primarily it's a form of contemplation." I agree. The processes of journal writing can offer you significant, highly effective spiritual support in a number of key ways.

Journal writing can offer you a way to:

~ Write or track your lifelong spiritual story
~ Create a place to talk to and listen to God, the Beloved, your Higher Self, or Inner Wisdom
~ Develop a sense of yourself as a soul, a divine spark
~ Reflect on Scripture or sacred writings

- Pray formally or, more often, informally
- Note prayers or insights that support your spiritual and psychological development
- Review and deepen your spiritual practice
- Frame your significant questions and explore them
- Identify and develop your understanding of your values
- Develop a way of seeing the world and other people with compassion and gratitude.

Using your journal to facilitate inner dialogue in this way, you will support your sense of inner reality and awareness. You will feel less reactive to what is happening outside yourself and thus less driven by it. You will also identify what may be inhibiting your spiritual growth and, most wonderfully, what supports it.

The intensity and interior focus of journal writing makes it an unparalleled tool for spiritual awakening and development. "I see myself differently because of journal writing," says Amelie. "But I also see other people differently and even the purpose of my life with much more confidence. Journal writing started out for me as a way of coping in a difficult time, but it is now my mirror. It reflects back to me what my concerns are, where I am going, and, most of all, what I need to pay attention to and know."

When I wrote via e-mail to the Universal Heart Network (www .stephaniedowrick.com) to suggest that people might like to send in their journal-writing experiences for this book, I was amazed and absolutely delighted by how many Networkers saw this aspect of journal writing as what matters to them most.

Here some of those journal writers describe this invaluable aspect of their journal writing.

Amada Doris

❝ My journal writing is my kind of authentic deep praying. I write at the end of my day when I am seated on my bed. I do not write every day. I write when something intense stirs my emotions. My journal always starts with 'Dear God, it's only me...' Or, 'Dear God, it's me again...' Or even just 'Dear God...' My journal is my way of talking to God, pouring out to Him everything that I feel about things that happen, or to thank Him for everything, every day. ❞

Robbie

❝ Journaling is always a part of my daily spiritual practice. It's not a matter of getting motivated to do it...it's that *without* the journaling I'm not motivated to cope calmly, serenely, and wisely with the myriad things a day brings along!

It's a conversation between me and God...I write and listen; He talks and listens. I use an ordinary spiral-bound exercise book (pages lay flat) and bin them as soon as they are full.

Conversation between me and God happens apart from journal writing, but I find it much, much easier to 'hear' during journal writing, partly because, I'm sure, by consciously concentrating on the quality of my thoughts enough to bother actually writing them down, I'm already doing a fair bit of 'quality control!'

I had just taken for granted that whenever I write in my journal I am writing to God, who is listening and will reply, and I write down whatever He says, and ask him to explain any bits I don't yet understand in a way that I can understand…and He does. But it hadn't occurred to me that this was happening only during journal writing until I began to pay closer attention to the actual process.

I notice that the 'conversation' takes quite a different form and tone during journal writing than, say, during voiced prayers. It is much more like spending time learning and being taught. I ask a lot of questions but not in a surly or whiney way (mainly!). I ask because I want to know for myself, direct from the source and not just another person's opinion.

There are many wonderful and learned voices in the world, but I know that I do not have the wisdom or knowledge to assay all their words…so I ask God, a lot, things like: Is this right for me? How do I put that into practical application? What does it mean in ordinary words? How come that learned opinion seems to directly clash with the other (different) opinions? Are they both wrong…are they both right? What, if any, is right for me and how do I apply that?

I've been journal writing for a long time, but over the last few years it has taken on a completely different quality. One day I just decided that I wanted to learn, and wanted to find out what God really thought about all manner of things, instead of just what I thought He was thinking (*ahem!*). And I decided to ask, prepared to accept His answer whether it agreed with 'my' theology or not! What a life-changing decision! 🙶 🙶

Some journal writers speak very directly to their journal. Debbie sees her journal as her "soul's companion." This is how she addresses her journal in describing its place in her life.

Debbie

❝ It is as though I invest a lifelike quality onto your coarse cream pages. I speak to you, with you, and you hold my thoughts, secrets, desires, my fears and apprehensions, and my shadow. You offer me another dimension of comfort and space, and a potential space for creativity and imagination.

You judge me not. With you I can be woman, child, mother, lover, real, phantasmic, strong or vulnerable, the dream teller, the dream reader, or the muse. You offer me a place to venture beyond the self, beyond the constraints of being.

More than 12 years ago, you began as a dream journal.

I was in the process of commencing practice as a psychotherapist in training. A dream awoke me through the voice of Elizabeth Jolley, a West Australian writer. She spoke to me as I was playing cello in a lovely music room in her home. *Write it down, it is a new score, new notes, and new thoughts.*

I was playing and hearing music I have no memory of hearing before.

So I began my Journal, and you became alive.

I occasionally revisit you and frequent places where nothing is ordinary. I am able to sit in the cool of my shadow and not be afraid, able to become poetic through the power of the written word, and able to give praise and be thankful for all the joy in my life.

The benefits of you as my soul's companion are endless. ❞

The spiritual insight or support that we are seeking through journal writing may at times be more muted and less direct.

Patricia's experience is that "God sends us what we need when we most need it." She had been a journal writer on and off for many years, but it wasn't until tragedy struck her family that she began to write more consistently.

Patricia

66 On May 27th last year, the day my husband Joe was diagnosed with multiple lesions on the brain, I began a journal. I pretty much wrote daily until his death, peacefully, at home, on April 28th this year.

I have read parts of it often, both during his illness and since his death, and shared parts of it, particularly his last month, with our children. Eventually I will give it all to them.

I tried to remain positive throughout, knowing that this was all the life we would have so we had to make the most of it. My journal doesn't sound too positive when I read, Friday, Sept. 2nd 12:30 a.m. 'Letting someone die at home always seemed such a noble dignified way to go, but Joe has no idea of what is happening and it is just messy, dirty, heartbreaking, constant hard work, and it has only just begun.' But it sometimes helps to face up to the truth.

I am only just beginning to feel just how hard it was, and I sometimes wonder if it wouldn't have been better to fall to pieces a bit more publicly every now and then, but then I realize that is not me. I feel that I was able to support not only Joe but our children, five of them, aged from 30 to 21, and their families, who were magnificent—each of them helped so wonderfully in their own special way—and his mum and brothers and sister.

[Later] I have since discovered that not only does it help to look back on what was happening on this day last month and the month before, but to keep on writing. **"**

Prayers and quotes

Writing out a prayer allows you to experience it far more deeply than if you simply read it and admire it. Quite recently I rediscovered a little prayer journal I had made for my daughter, Kezia, when she was ten. Some of the prayers I wrote myself; others I took from different traditions. It has become even more precious because in those pages Kezia wrote some prayers of her own in the form of letters to God. Again, no photo could possibly convey the sweetness of the memories evoked by what she wrote and even her childlike handwriting.

Here is one of the prayers that I wrote out for her (and, breaking my own rules, didn't source):

Within God's hand
I lay my soul,
Both when I sleep
And when I wake.
And with my soul,
my body, too.
The Lord is close.
I shall not fear.

Rereading that prayer is already a pleasure, but far more potent are the memories that it aroused for me in what I intended for Kezia as I wrote it out: "*Within God's hand, I lay my soul.*"

Creating a prayer journal is one of the simplest and loveliest ways to ensure a steady stream of inspiration. It affords a form of contemplation that can be central to your devotional practice.

And if prayer is not of interest to you, the same method can be used for inspirational sayings that are not explicitly spiritual.

I was ordained as an Interfaith Minister in 2005 and now offer regular Interfaith services in my home city, Sydney, as well as continuing Interfaith retreats in other parts of the country and overseas. My prayer journal, which is actually a ring-bound folder filled with references, printouts, photocopies, handwritten prayers, and, increasingly, the prayers that I write myself, has become a resource for me, supplementing the many books I have on prayer and spiritual practice.

My inclination is to find prayers or inspirational sayings that speak to my heart and highest aspirations from many sources and traditions. I am drawn by the quality of the thought; its family of origin is less crucial to me. You may want to explore your own tradition more exclusively, and one of the loveliest ways to do this is to ask people who share your tradition to offer their favorite prayers. Some of the prayers in Kezia's homemade prayer book were given to me many years ago by a young Jewish man who came to one of my talks in Britain (after *Intimacy & Solitude* was published there), recognized my interest in his spiritual journey, and then wrote out for me his favorite prayers. Sharing those with me, written on a gray sheet of paper in his own handwriting, he shared something very wonderful about his interior life and faith and what sustains it.

Part of my spiritual story is also indirectly recorded in my journal entries where I reflect on the choices of my children's names, where I recorded in careful detail my son Gabriel's first "big questions" and his innocent and wondrous curiosity about his place in the world, where I prayed for both my children as they grew, where I described times of difficulty and even anguish, where I drew support and consolation from the people closest to me, where I recorded small but valuable insights and joys.

ॐ
Writing your spiritual story

I saw the other side of Colombo going out to the
Katunayake airport. There were many screwy Catholic
statues exhibited in public but sometimes under glass,
so that the Catholic saints come a little closer to Ganesha
and Hindu camp after all. Suddenly there is a point
where religion becomes laughable. Then you decide
that you are nevertheless religious.

—Thomas Merton, *The Asian Journals*

A spiritual autobiography or story is not always a story of faith.
It can be a story of false turns and inspiration, contradictions
and confusion. It can be a story of hilarity as well as sorrow. It
may reflect a tentative sense of being connected to life's mystery
and more robustly recognizing our inevitable connections with
one another. Pierre Teilhard de Chardin, a twentieth-century
French priest and writer, suggested that we are not human beings
having spiritual experiences but spiritual beings having a human
experience. Does that resonate with you?

I don't know whether I believe in God or not....
But the essential thing is to put oneself in a frame of mind
which is close to that of prayer.

—Henri Matisse

The exercise that follows is really many exercises in one. Your reflection and writing may continue over many months or years. You may even want to select a special journal just for this theme.

Your turn
✒ Your spiritual story

AS YOU START

Take your time writing your spiritual story. Part of coming more alive spiritually is tuning in instinctively to what is helpful to pursue and what is not.

Each time you write more of your spiritual story, take at least twenty to thirty minutes to write without any interruptions.

You may want to light a candle, and perhaps meditate for a short while before writing. You may want to play some uplifting or calming music.

You may also want to comment in your "usual" journal (if you are writing your spiritual story separately) on how this process is developing.

CONTINUE WITH

Choose just *one* question or prompt at any one time as your focus. But if your thoughts or memories take you on to other topics, follow those inner promptings.

Where does your spiritual story begin?

What kind of spiritual environment were you born into?

Recall when you first became aware that you are more than mind and body? And what has continued to remind you of this?

Explore the key spiritual landmarks of your childhood, early adulthood, later adulthood (events, teachings, teachers, insights, books).

Recall three or four significant spiritual insights or experiences from each decade of your life and describe them in detail. Think about how they affected you then and now. Are they still resonating?

Do you recall prayers from childhood? Or particular teachings that were significant?

What feeds you, spiritually? (Return to this often.)

Think about some losses and what you eventually learned or gained from them.

Have you been hurt by people in the name of religion? Or are there teachings from the past that have limited you or given you a distorted picture of yourself? If your answer is yes, take time to write about these. Perhaps write letters in your journal that *you do not send to the people involved*. You may want to comfort the child or young person you once were. You can write to your past self also, offering compassion and understanding. This can be powerfully effective.

What does *acting with spiritual integrity* mean to you? Think about the people you know who do act with consistent integrity. Can you describe what is most impressive or inspiring about them?

Who are your spiritual heroes? Who are your guides/teachers/role models? Think about their qualities and write about what they have given you. How can you live out those qualities in your own life? And appreciate them more in other people?

Think about some helpful "coincidences" that have occurred in your life or times when "just by chance" the right person, book, phrase, prayer, insight dropped into your lap.

Write in detail about as many "epiphany" moments as you can recall and open yourself to noticing and writing about more.

"Feeling alive" is a powerful phrase. Does it have any special spiritual meaning for you?

There is great spirituality and unity to be discovered in beauty, including the natural beauty of the world around us. Explore that in relation to your daily life.

The great spiritual qualities are kindness, compassion, tolerance, forgiveness, and—greatest of all—love. They are your spiritual inheritance. How are you claiming them?

Take some time to write about some of the biggest hurdles in your life and especially what you learned from them.

Take some time to write about some of the biggest joys in your life and what you learned from them.

Explore silence and what it can give you.

Make a list over several weeks of the words or thoughts that people have said that have really *helped*.

Make a list over several weeks of what you believe your major life-shifting insights have been. Some may have come from people who had a negative effect on your life but, nevertheless, taught you something of value.

What are your spiritual goals? Whom will they benefit?

What do you most want to give to others?

How could your thoughts about spirituality deepen your appreciation of life?

GENERAL ENCOURAGEMENT

Let your spiritual story "brew" slowly. As your attention to it deepens, you will be delighted with what memories and insights you discover. You may also find that you feel much more alive in all kinds of ways. The Sufi poet Rumi reminds you, "Your soul is here for its own joy."

Writing the facts

Take time for quiet reflection and gratitude for what you are discovering and recording.

Complete this sentence: "My insight for today is…"

Let your thoughts "rest."

One of the many unsung benefits of journal writing is that it provides a context in which clarity and focus can be developed. In a world where our attention is pulled in many directions, and where much of what we pay attention to is rushed, superficial, and unsatisfying, developing an authentic capacity to concentrate, focus, and reflect becomes priceless. Writing your thoughts down already brings far more insight than "mulling them over" ever could. Quiet persistence is also something that journal writing supports: returning to a knotty issue as often as you need to until you understand it better and then, wiser, can move on.

In this book I have also repeatedly emphasized how supportive of your well-being it is to identify and ask your questions. Taking the time to clarify what your question is and allowing it to "work" in your mind, rather than rushing at the "answer" closest to hand, is also very much part of the reflective processes that underpin creative journal writing.

Robbie uses her journal very explicitly for spiritual training, believing it is necessary to bring concentration and focus to our spiritual development as well as good intentions. That makes sense. Without focus, and especially without seeing clearly how to translate insight into practice, how to let *our thoughts make a difference*, "spiritual development" or psychological development remains not much more than a nice idea.

Robbie

66 I find clarity through circling around a subject and looking at and considering all its aspects. It comes by a state of mental concentration and of truly focusing on our thoughts and feelings and paying attention. And clarity is not something you just arrive at, and then there it is—clarity for life! It is a constant refining process. Because if we are growing and developing, there is always a bigger picture than the one we had before. Our vision is being constantly enlarged.

There is a lot of "pop psychology" among the self-development and self-growth literature that encourages folks to "get out of their heads," and this is part of the holistic process, too. But it has also bred almost a fear of concentration and focus…a fear of thinking. It's all too easy to have a vague idea of how we would like to make a difference to the world! But from vague thought comes vague action! Self-growth, self-development, and spirituality are not mindless! It is all about wholeness and graceful balance (the unity of the whole), but how balanced can it be if we leave our intelligence out of the marriage of intellect *and* intuition? 99

Your turn
●○ Ask God the question

If you could ask God (the Divine, the Supreme Soul, the Universe) any question, what would it be? *Write it down.*

And whenever you feel moved to do so, let yourself write an answer.

Your turn
✦➤ *Listening to your soul*

One of the most important relationships in your life is with your soul. Will you be kind and loving to your soul, or will you be harsh and difficult?

—Elisabeth Kübler-Ross

AS YOU START

Before you begin to think and write, light a candle, put on some relaxing music, sit comfortably, and quiet your mind. You are honoring the sacred within.

CONTINUE WITH

Choose just one of the topics below as your starting point for a letter, or series of letters, from your soul to you.

Which of your current spiritual practices feel nourishing? Could you make more room for those in your life? How will you achieve that?

What does your soul "long for"? Let your soul tell you clearly what that is and how you will achieve it.

Which soul qualities or strengths would support you to live more closely in tune with the Divine, with your own life, your highest spiritual aspirations; with greater tolerance and acceptance for all of humanity?

How does your life's purpose look from your soul's perspective?

What are your soul's gifts to this world?

What would enable you to see "the soul" in other people and respond accordingly?

GENERAL ENCOURAGEMENT

This is a topic that you may want to return to a number of times. It is well worth returning to whenever you feel inwardly "dry," or cut off from other people or yourself. It returns you to your deepest and most sustaining sense of who and what you are.

Write for at least twenty to thirty minutes.

END WITH

Finish by completing this sentence: "My soul has told me…"

Don't reread immediately.

Let your thoughts "rest."

Your turn
✏ Six hundred minutes of thanks

Spend ten minutes *each day for sixty days* writing down what you have to be thankful for.

Set yourself a target for what you will notice, starting with five things a day and working up to…fifty!

This is an exercise that is wonderful to share with your whole family or community. Children of all ages love it, and living as we do in a culture of insufficiency and complaint, it is stirring and powerful spiritually and psychologically.

You can make some of your "gratitudes" public, writing them on cards and putting them up on the fridge, talking about them, sending notes to friends.

After sixty days, write an account in your journal of how this exercise has changed your perspective on life and on yourself.

Forgiveness

Forgiveness is a tough topic but an essential one to think about in the context of spiritual awareness and development. I have written a book, *Forgiveness & Other Acts of Love*, that arose out of my own need to understand forgiveness and the other universal qualities that enable us to become fully ourselves and to live with compassion for other people. You may want to read that or any other book on forgiveness and then write at length about your own views on this extremely challenging topic.

   The exercise that follows will give you most when you make it highly specific to your own situation, describing that situation in detail in your journal, looking for what is not resolved, asking questions, and gradually allowing greater illumination to come forward from your own pages.

Your turn
Forgiveness

AS YOU START
Before you begin to think and write, light a candle, put on some relaxing music, sit comfortably, and quiet your mind.

CONTINUE WITH
Choose any one of the topics below as your starting point, always bringing it back to the experiences of your own life.

Forgiving *yourself*, learning, moving on.

Distinguishing between what upsets you and what injures you.

Forgiving others or letting go of the wish that they might suffer.

Accepting others' forgiveness of the harm you may have caused.

Forgiving God, or life itself, for the hurts that have come your way.

Moving on, clear about what you have learned.

What are the lessons forgiveness needs to bring to your life?

GENERAL ENCOURAGEMENT

Each time you write on this topic, spend at least twenty to thirty minutes writing, looking with compassion at your situation and that of any others involved.

Explore your attitudes, thoughts, and feelings.

Note what is helpful.

It may also help you to ask, "How would ____ deal with this?" thinking about the person you most admire for their spiritual depth and stability.

END WITH

Finish this sentence: "I am grateful to see that…"

Let your thoughts "rest."

Write to your wise self

Whenever you need to know more than your conscious mind is telling you, you can use your journal as a place to write to your inner Wise Being or Self in as much detail as you can. You can follow a letter format, or simply pour your thoughts onto the page.

Don't expect insight, clarity or "answers" immediately. Journal writing is about process, not instant answers!

You can trust, however, that greater clarity will come. Perhaps when you are standing in the supermarket checkout line over-hearing someone else's conversation; perhaps next time you open a favorite book, perhaps next time someone asks *you* for advice and you hear yourself saying something useful or profound.

Journal writing encourages you to trust your inner life, the value of your own experiences and reflections, and the precious fragments of your own inner wisdom.

Truly, it is in the darkness that one finds light, so when we are in sorrow, then this light is nearest of all to us.

—Meister Eckhart

Giving great peace and happiness to others is completely up to you because it depends upon what you do with your mind.

—Lama Zopa Rinpoche

Kerry has used journal writing for some years to dialogue with her inner child to heal some of the grief and shame that she felt from childhood. To her surprise those conversations with her inner child "became more and more spiritual in nature."

Kerry

66 She became my guide and teacher, supporting and encouraging me through hard times, challenging and confronting me at other times. She invited me to open my heart and deeply love.

Looking back on those times I am amazed at the patience, constancy, and love that is expressed through my conversations with [her inner child]. The relationship is very personal, and although the written dialogues are fewer now than before, the relationship is strong and inspirational, rich with metaphor and insight, always inviting me to travel further and deeper into the mystery of the divine. 99

Laden with treasures . . .

To write is to sit and stare, hypnotized, at
the reflection of the window in the silver
inkstand, to feel the divine fever mounting
to one's cheeks and forehead while the hand
that writes grows blissfully numb upon the
paper. It also means idle hours curled up in
the hollow of the divan, and then an orgy of
inspiration, from which one emerges stupefied
and aching all over, but already recompensed,
and laden with treasures that one unloads
slowly onto the virgin page in the little round
pool of light under the lamp.

—Colette, *The Vagabond*

Your life in your journal

More writing
and writing more

There will be days when you open your journal and find that it writes itself. This is how Leslie describes that experience.

Leslie

❝I started off by recording whatever event in the day felt most unfinished. I could have chosen what was most interesting or surprising or maybe complicated. But for me 'unfinished' was the thing most likely to keep me awake at night and make me feel small or helpless. What I would always find though is that one thing led to another. I might start with a problem from work, for example, and then find I was writing about something I remembered from another situation entirely.

I love the times when the writing flows like that and makes its own jumps from one thing to another. It's always unpredictable why it will do that. It's not about being tired or having more energy. It just happens.❞

There may be times when journal writing "comes to the rescue," as Bernadette describes it here.

Bernadette

❝On March 29 this year I broke my left ankle, getting off a bus at Ashfield station on the way to work. 7:30 a.m. Clean break to lower fibula, the hospital confirmed, just near the ankle joint. After 6 weeks in plaster, I was glad to be able to put my two feet on the ground again on May 9. But then began the excruciating recovery: how to persuade that foot to walk normally? How long would it take?

On April 9, 1990, I broke my right ankle trying to ice-skate at a joint birthday celebration. *Perhaps my journal from then could help chart the journey?*

But no. All I'd written then was: 'June 23, ankle very sore. Will I really manage to be crutch-free next week?' April 9 to June 23: more than 2 months! How am I going to walk properly on our Vietnam holiday from June 19 [this year]?

But journal writing has come to the rescue again.

This time I am charting each minute daily improvement: 'ankle rotation, bigger circles; wall stretch x 20, less pain; turned in shower, hands free; lump on shin softer tonight.'

By week three I am walking slowly without crutches and nudging through the objecting creaks in my lower foot. And I have found patience in the healing. I am sure I'll enjoy Vietnam as well.❞

There may also be times when you need an established routine to call on to get started, to get started yet again, or to sustain you. This is often the case when you are entering difficult new emotional terrain. Perhaps you are allowing yourself to be more honest than you have been previously. (Journal writing will make you more honest and by so doing will provide you with a healing sense of integrity and wholeness.)

Perhaps you are writing about tough issues, like disappointment, a heartache or loss, or forgiveness. Or it may be that your self-confidence is low and you feel that you have only your commitment to your journal to sustain you.

In my professional writing life I know that I often feel astonishingly physically restless when my mind is reaching toward something but I am not ready to write about it. Or when I am about to write something that is emotionally challenging and I feel inadequate and uncertain. At those times I pace my office, taking books off my shelves and reading brief snatches of other people's writing before my mind darts on to something else. Or I leave my office altogether and go for long, speedy walks. Or I drift around clothes shops or art galleries in a kind of daze while some part of my mind continues to work on what is actually engaging me. In those restless, unsettled, and unsettling times I am also likely to feel extremely hungry, needing something tough or crunchy to get my "teeth into."

Writing in my journal doesn't raise those kinds of anxieties for me. The privacy of the journal protects me. In the journal, I am never thinking about what others will make of what I am writing. I am not explaining or trying to clarify things for them, only for myself. My shortfalls when it comes to journal writing are setting it aside for too long or even entirely neglecting it because the demands of my other writing can feel so pressing. However, I do know that the anxieties I experience in other areas of my writing can certainly plague journal writers. The lovely thing is, though, that within the context of journal writing it is possible to *start with those observations* and incorporate them into whatever else you are writing. ("I vaguely thought I would like to be writing about

Geoff and his problems with his dad, but something's getting in the way, and after three cups of coffee, when I never drink coffee, I feel like I am spinning off the planet, which may be where I would rather be.")

The portable journal

Enjoy how *portable* your journal is.

You can write it in cafés, on the train, late at night or before dawn, silently in your room.

Right here, right now?

Observing what is going on in the present moment (and not just what happened earlier in the day or week) is integral to journal writing. What's more, observing what is going on *right now* can be far more direct and even more truthful than recording experiences that are somewhat obscured by the mists of time. It may be that your focus is on the past, but you can still look at it in the clear light of the present moment. ("When I get distracted by all the old resentment about Geoff and his dad, I need to ask myself why this old itch is pushing its way in now. I want to think about Geoff's sense of duty toward his dad in a bigger context, and maybe that conversation I had with Patsy today is one way in.")

Curiosity is key here. Observe whatever is happening in your thoughts or feelings with interest. You are observing to find out more and not to judge or criticize. Keeping to your routine of writing, and observing *the process of writing* with as much interest as the content of your days, gives you an invaluable sense of inner stability, even at times of uncertainty.

This was Helena's experience.

Helena

❝My promise to myself was to write in my journal at least every second day. I wrote that promise into the front of my journal, and I've kept to it, too, except on a couple of occasions. Some days I just make a note of what is strongest in my mind. More often though I try to develop at least one issue further by writing for half an hour or so. If I have real difficulties with it, then I take it as a signal that this is a knotty issue for me. That is, when I am slowed up, I know there will be a reason for that, so I investigate what's going on. I ask myself questions like 'Is this familiar?' or 'How would this look a month or a year from now?' Or I might just jot down all the feelings and associations I have with the particular issue. Then I often leave it to 'brew.' I have told my subconscious that I'm interested; then I wait for a response. Sometimes I have to wait a while, but there will always come a dream, or a rush of writing, or just a sudden insight that gives me more information than diligent, linear writing ever could.❞

The blank page

For many professional writers, the blank page is a nightmare. For creative journal writers, the fresh page can be an invitation, a letter unopened from yourself to yourself. Each time you begin to write, start exactly where you are.

Place. Time. Date.
Some brief notes about the atmosphere/climate/sounds.
Thoughts.
Feelings.
How your body feels. What your body is "telling" you.

Then, when you are easily and inevitably warmed up, keep writing.
Free-associate.
Free-write.
Incorporate your observations of this moment and your response to it in whatever else you are writing.

Writing about "nothing"

"Nothing" has a big part to play in journal writing. "Nothing" is often where "something" is hiding. Similarly, "nowhere" may take you to the perfect "somewhere." Christopher Robin and Winnie-the-Pooh describe this magnificently in A. A. Milne's *The House at Pooh Corner*:

"Where are we going?" said Pooh, hurrying after [Christopher Robin]....

"Nowhere," said Christopher Robin.

So they began going there and after they had walked a little way Christopher Robin said, "What do you like doing best in the world, Pooh?"

"Well," said Pooh, "what I like best—" and then he had to stop and think about eating honey, visiting Christopher Robin, being with Piglet, humming along....

"I like that too," said Christopher Robin, "but what I like doing best is Nothing."

"How do you do Nothing?" asked Pooh, after he wondered for a long time.

"Well, it's when people call out at you as you're going off to do it, 'What are you going to do, Christopher Robin?' and you say, 'Oh, nothing,' and then you go and do it."

"Oh, I see," said Pooh.

"This is a nothing sort of thing that we're doing now."

"Oh, I see," said Pooh again.

"It means just going along, listening to all the things you can't hear, and not bothering."

"Oh!" said Pooh.

Exploring "nothing"

All too often people say, "I'd like to write a journal, but I am afraid that I would have nothing to say." As Manesh shows, this is rarely true.

Manesh

❝I did keep a diary for years, but it was just a shorthand account of events. I read other people's journals like [those of] Anaïs Nin, Katherine Mansfield, Anne Frank. And of course, Boswell and Proust. I found their diaries far more interesting than reading novels or biographies, and maybe it was because their insights were so exquisite, it intimidated me. My life felt frankly dull next to theirs. But the funny thing was that it was only when I got going and started to write what I call my 'real' journal that I could also see that many of the things that those greats paid attention to were also trivial and unremarkable in and of themselves. They became beautiful or meaningful because they were being noticed.

What made a difference for me funnily enough was studying still-life painting as a hobby. The objects we painted were everyday objects, as is often true with still life. One day though I could see the connection that seems so obvious now between journal writing and still-life painting. Both art forms—and I regard them as art—invite you to pause. What I am recording when I write in my journal are a whole series of pauses, and really and truly nothing else is needed.❞

One of the most effective ways to write a lot about "something" is to try to force yourself to write about "nothing!" (Try now, for a moment, to think about "nothing" and discover how difficult or impossible it is.) This is partly because *nothing* always has a particular subjective meaning. It is also because we humans are incurably and wonderfully contrary.

Even when we are aware that an instruction is "paradoxical" ("Do NOT think of a yellow canary"), our minds grab on to paradoxical suggestions and begin to play without further prompting.

Often "nothing" is a kind of veil: we need to draw it aside and look behind it to find out where "something" is hiding. Sometimes "nothing" is also a defense against feeling or even against thinking. It can even be a kind of passive aggression that shuts other people out or punishes them.

"What's wrong?"
"Nothing."
"Can I help?"
"No."
"Is there anything that I can do for you?"
"Probably not."

When "nothing" dulls your mind, take at least as much interest in what's going on as when you are filled with ideas and eager to write. This will give you a dramatic demonstration of how thoughts are really energy forms. (And the quality of what we are thinking will always affect us as well as other people.) As you write, the energy of "nothing" will quite inevitably change into something else. You will feel it, not simply perceive it.

Your turn
━━━ Lots about nothing

AS YOU START
Note the day and time, and describe where you are sitting to write and how you are feeling. (That's already quite a lot of "something.")

Sit for a while longer with "nothing." Taste it. Get the flavor of this particular experience. Be aware of what's going on in your body.

Any of the prompts that follow can support you to find out more about "nothing."

If you notice strong emotions or associations arising as you write, include them in your writing. ("Dad was the one who was always on our backs to do something however boring it was. I hated that, but I drive myself by keeping busy also and even writing in this diary, when surely there is SOMETHING that is far more important to be doing, still causes me to feel anxious sometimes as though NOTHING I do just for myself is really SOMETHING of value.")

CONTINUE WITH

Choose instinctively from the following prompts. Return to the same topic until you are confident that you really have got something out of "nothing."

"'Nothing' right now feels like…"

"Buried inside 'nothing' is…"

"'Nothing' is a big blanket that lets me hide from…"

"I hate it when I ask people what's wrong and they say, 'Nothing.'"

"I'm the kind of person who will say that nothing's wrong when it isn't true."

"I like to be clear about everything at least a day/month/ year in advance."

"You're a big NOTHING…"

"The best time I ever had doing nothing was when…"

"I often feel I have nothing to contribute when…"

"If 'nothing' could smell, it would smell like…"

"If 'nothing' had a taste, it would be..."

"If I were to hold 'nothing' in my hands, it would feel like..."

"Nothing and nowhere are lonely experiences for me."

"The devil makes work for idle hands."

"I envy people who have time to do nothing..."

"I have too much 'nothing' in my life."

"I don't know whether 'nothing' is an outside experience or an inside one. What it's like for me is..."

END WITH

Finish this sentence: "'Nothing' turned into..."

Relish your imagination and good humor.

Some practical suggestions

✎ **"Nothing" is a first reaction, a defense.** Regard it with curiosity. Go into it. Don't be put off.

✎ **"Nothing" often has a shape.** Observe that shape inside your mind with your eyes closed. Then observe whether that shape changes and becomes something else. Then write about it.

✎ **Try dialoguing with nothing.** *What are you? Where have you come from? What do you want to tell me?* Write down both sides of the conversation. Listen carefully to "nothing!"

Unfinished business

There is still much about me that I dislike; and yet I feel already that these qualities are foreign, contingent, not really connected to me. From this comes…a certain strength.

—Rainer Maria Rilke, *Diaries of a Young Poet*

We all have it: unfinished business. One of the greatest gifts journal writing can offer is the chance not necessarily to "finish" that business but to understand it (and ourselves) better. Isabelle talks about her "unfinished business" like this.

Isabelle

66I was raised by my grandmother, and she died when I was 17. I had some counseling in my twenties and thirties, but I can honestly say that one of the best things I ever did was writing a series of letters to Nan over a period of about eight months. I did it after I lost a close friend of my own age and felt terribly confronted by death all over again. I had really blamed myself that I was horrible to Nan in the year before she died and that I didn't do enough for my friend Danny either. That guilt is still with me but not in anything like the same way. I probably wrote about nine or ten letters in all. I've never reread them, but I honestly felt like Nan knew exactly what I was saying to her. I spoke to her through my heart, and it was astonishingly releasing. I've got the letters in my journal, and it's almost like having a communication there from her, even though I wrote them.❞

Unfinished business quite often gets finished in the pages of a journal. Or it becomes the rich soil where something else grows, and then it simply fades from your attention.

Unfinished business tends to stay around when there are forgiveness issues or regrets. Sometimes "closure" is not possible. (I am not even entirely sure what closure is.) Often "acceptance" is enough. Or else the sense of "moving on" with greater understanding.

When unfinished business feels pressing or doesn't go away, there are a number of ways that your journal writing can help you, not always to "finish" necessarily but perhaps to have rather more insight and a greater feeling of choice.

Before you look at one situation in particular, you may want to explore whether "finishing" generally is an issue for you. In what circumstances is it easier? Can you borrow some insights from those more positive situations?

You may also want to explore what lies beyond "finished." Write out in a great deal of detail the scenario that best describes the situation being finished or resolved—or moved on from. Write it in the present tense, tuning in to your senses as though what you envision has already happened. ("I am now living in a small house on my own. It is very quiet and the furniture doesn't quite match in the long corridor-shaped sitting room, and I like that. Even more I like the array of squat pots outside my door, where I am growing a huge variety of fresh herbs and sometimes I eat them for breakfast they smell so good: basil on toast. Delicious. With tomatoes on the side.")

CREATIVE JOURNAL WRITING

"Finishing"—like journal writing itself—has its own integrity and inner timetable. Your conscious mind can want something to be decisively over and finished with, yet your unconscious mind may still be worrying away at it. Writing about a complex situation is a highly effective way to bring those conscious and unconscious processes closer together, especially when you can do so without feeling that things must be resolved in a particular way or within a particular time frame. Marion Woodman, a Jungian analyst and writer, expresses this very forcefully when she says, "Journal writing is crucial to recognizing those parts of ourselves that we have shunned. Unconsciousness needs the eye of consciousness."

Joe found writing a letter—inside his journal and *not for posting*—surprisingly helpful.

Joe

66 Two years after my marriage ended, I wrote a long letter to my ex-wife in my journal to try to heal some of my pain. I wrote it and then put it away for about a month. I couldn't even bear to get the journal out during that time. When I did get it out again I wrote another draft. This went on for several more weeks. What I discovered was that I had to forgive myself more than my wife. We are both good people who got caught up in a spiral that said a lot about our inexperience. She left me for someone else, and that was devastating. But my capacity to be a loving partner had also got lost along the way. In that way, I'd also left her. Writing about it also brought back the good times that I had kind of forgotten. It was extremely hard to do, but yes, certainly worth it. And no, I didn't ever post the letter. It didn't seem right to do so. I'm moving on. 99

Your turn
Unfinished business

AS YOU START

Note the date and the time of day, and how you are feeling.

Describe clearly for yourself what your unfinished business is.

(This may be all you need to do. Often identifying what it is feels "enough.")

CONTINUE WITH

Take all the time you need to reflect on your "unfinished business."

You may want to deal just with the easiest aspect of it.

You may want to start by "free-associating": allowing a string of words to jump from your mind onto the page.

When you notice that you are judging or criticizing yourself, write that into your journal and move on.

You could also ask yourself what "finishing this business" would feel like. Sometimes old worries or torments are familiar and have their uses. But generally, they also have a use-by date. It's liberating to know when that is.

GENERAL ENCOURAGEMENT

You can explore your unfinished business in a number of ways. Choose instinctively from those below. You may need to be patient as well as persistent.

Describe the situation in detail. Write several "ideal resolutions." Does anything need doing that would take you closer to one of them?

Describe the situation to your inner Wise Being or Higher Self. Be very clear about what you don't understand or what feels unresolved. Then write a reply from your Wise Being.

Write a letter or a series of letters either to the person involved or to the situation itself. Do NOT post these letters. *They belong in your journal.*

Write a letter to yourself from the point of view of anyone else involved.

Write a letter of advice to yourself from the perspective of someone whose wisdom you value.

END WITH

Finish this sentence: "I am glad to discover that…"

This time, really do let your thoughts "rest." Trust that when you begin to write again you will know more than you do now.

Some practical suggestions

✎ **Move slowly.** There may be deep emotions swirling around, some of them unconscious. Treat yourself compassionately.

✎ **Start by doing nothing more than describing in your journal what your unfinished business is.** Later on you may choose to record what attempts you have already made to get more insight. And what benefits you have gained.

✎ **Identify and record what your hopes are.** ("I want to be able to think about this much less." "I want to feel confident that I have done the best I can to…")

✎ **Look objectively at the obstacles that lie between you and that outcome.** Are they self-made? What differences can you make through a shift in attitude, a bigger perspective, greater insight, or changed behaviors?

Let problems "rest"

I suspect that we are all sometimes guilty of running around asking other people what we should be doing with our lives, assuming they know more about us than we do. In creative journal writing, you can "ask your journal," a very effective way to access that wiser part of yourself. It is useful to write out your question in fairly precise detail and then leave it rather than grasp at the first answer that comes to mind.

In much the same way, your journal can be an ideal place to "rest" a problem, trusting your unconscious mind to sort it out and giving your conscious mind a welcome break.

"Solutions" don't have to be instant. Sometimes they can't be. We often grasp for an instant solution to relieve our anxiety and find we are in worse trouble. Letting a problem "rest," and trusting that, gives you exceptional possibilities to allow worthwhile insights to develop.

Letting problems "rest" can also create invaluable boundaries so that you think about your problem only while you are writing about it and not otherwise. (It can't ruin your entire day.)

As with "unfinished business," it helps to write out in detail what the issue is. ("I can't decide whether to give up this job, which is boring but safe, or risk the new job even though that's for three months only.") It may even be appropriate at this point to write out what the positives are for each or every possible decision. You may want to do this as a list. You can also do it as a letter to your journal, convincing your journal of one viewpoint and then the other. ("Dear Journal, I know that job security is more important to me than anything else, and as I am thirty-five and have a mortgage, no one could argue with that.")

Throughout this book, at the end of the exercises, I have suggested that you let your thoughts "rest." This is because I know how dispiriting it is to keep worrying about something unproductively and because I also trust the unconscious to do some of the wisdom work for you.

Your turn
☛ "Resting" a problem

AS YOU START

Note the date, time, and place of your writing. ("3:00 a.m. Can't sleep, so may as well write.")

Note your state of mind right now.

Take time to state clearly what the problem is. *Start afresh each time you write about it.*

You may want to deal just with the easiest aspect of it or start by "free-associating," allowing a string of words to jump from your mind onto the page.

CONTINUE WITH

Write about the emotions you associate with this kind of problem. ("Feel worse because my friends are all happily settled in their jobs, and I don't begrudge them that, but…")

Reflect, and then write in detail about what you hope for. ("Just want to be able to set it aside. I can see clearly how…")

Pay close attention to what's going on in your body, and write about that. Often that pain in the back, or the cold in your hands, tells a little story in itself.

Write for at least twenty minutes.

No stopping to edit or rewrite.

You may also want to:

Look at the problem from the perspective of a year from now, then five years from now. Will it matter? To whom? And how? Write in as much detail as you can.

Imagine how the wisest person you know—or know of— would deal with this issue or problem. Write about that in detail. Or write yourself a letter, as if from that person.

Write a letter to your journal about the problem.

Write about the problem in the third person. ("Francine thinks she wants to retire early.")

Write about what it would feel like if this problem was never solved, just survived.

Experiment with this train of thought: "I would prefer to have this problem solved, but it is not essential."

END WITH

Finish by completing this sentence: "Now I can see that..."

Let your thoughts, and the problem, "rest."

The opposite
may also be true

The two hardest things to handle in life
are failure and success.

—Anonymous

Many years ago, when I was doing my earliest training in psycho-therapy, we were asked to do an apparently simple little exercise that basically consisted of looking at a few cards drawn from a tarot pack and then describing one card in great detail from a negative and then from a positive point of view. As you may have guessed, the point of the exercise was to challenge the way that all of us fall into the rut of our own lazy assumptions! Most of us routinely think in divisive ways (good/bad, black/white). We find it hard to remember that most situations are complex and contain all kinds of elements—favorable and less favorable—depending on your perspective.

Many painful, difficult, or "tricky" situations can be eased wonderfully if you approach them—with your creative journal-writing mind and in the pages of your journal—less defensively and with greater openness and curiosity.

Seeing "all sides of the story" won't turn you into a wishy-washy person, but it may make you a wiser one. You may even have the same point of view as when you started, but you will be less aggressive about it and more flexible. And where you can concede a point, or understand where someone else is coming from, in most situations you will find that their attitude will also soften.

Somehow this quote from Robert Fulghum expresses that bigness of mind for me. "Some Sunday mornings," he wrote, "you'll find me at the Greek Orthodox church, even though I am neither Greek nor Orthodox.... I am consciously putting myself into a place where richness comes to me in a way that's beyond words."

Your turn
➤ Four sides to the story

AS YOU START

Note where and when you are writing. ("On the ferry. Night is cold and wet.")

Note your state of mind right now. ("This feels like very thin ice....Mad thing to say while the ferry is rocking.")

Take a few moments to reflect on any complex situation where you feel somewhat "stuck" or rather more entrenched and limited than a creative journal writer ought to be!

Identify what you need or want: solution, inspiration, fresh perspective, flexibility, or courage.

CONTINUE WITH

Keep noting your emotions and thoughts, and the hopes that arise as you begin to reflect.

You may want to start by "free-associating," allowing a string of words to jump from your mind onto the page.

Be aware of what's going on in your body.

Try to write for at least twenty minutes.

No stopping to edit or rewrite.

FOUR STEPS

You may choose to take only one step at a time. No problem! This may be very wise. Once again, it's the process that counts. Any "result" is a bonus.

1. Describe whatever situation you have chosen from your own totally subjective point of view. Give yourself time to reflect on the issue. Get down every point that will support your view. Explore the emotions that are driving your arguments. Write down why this matters so much to you. Feel entitled!

2. Now write about your desired outcome. What will it achieve? What will it do for you? Write about it in the present tense *as though it has happened*. ("I am so thrilled that I finally managed to convince Ted to go on holiday.")

3. Now write about the outcome as though you did not get what you were hoping for. What will that be like for you? Write about it in the present tense *as though it has happened*. ("I never did manage to convince Ted to go on holiday, and it seems like this is the last time that I want to concede something so important to me.")

4. Now write about the situation from the point of view of whoever else is involved. Take your time with this. Sit like that person. Use their language. Try to get thoroughly "in character" physically as well as mentally. Take on that person's attitudes as wholeheartedly as if they were your own. Inhabit them. ("I hate seeing Margie so angry, but I feel like neither one of us has room to say what we really want without offending the other one.")

You may also want to write a "letter" in this journal either to someone else involved or to the situation itself. ("Dear Ideal Holiday...") Don't mail it or even talk about it, especially

CREATIVE JOURNAL WRITING

not until you are quite sure that you are not attacking or self-justifying.

If you are very troubled by difficult emotions, try allowing yourself to identify what the "opposite" emotion might be. Explore what an abundance of that emotion would give you. ("I am not sure if acceptance is the opposite of resentment; maybe I am looking for a sense of freedom rather than resignation, or even assertiveness, now I come to think about it. And for me, and maybe for Ted, too, a bit more clarity and assertiveness would allow…")

GENERAL ENCOURAGEMENT

Let yourself write instinctively and freely, especially when you are taking yourself into new territory. If you notice strong emotions or associations arising as you write, include them in your writing as you go. If something really "gets you going," it is worth writing about.

Don't edit or rewrite.

END WITH

Write out your most stunning insight. Underline it!

Let your thoughts "rest."

Recording quotations and comments

For some of us, books are as important as almost anything else on earth. What a miracle it is that out of these small, flat, rigid squares of paper unfolds world after world, worlds that sing to you, comfort and quiet or excite you.... Books are full of all the things that you don't get in real life— wonderful, lyrical language, for instance, right off the bat.

—Anne Lamott, *Bird by Bird*

I suspect that most journal writers are also keen readers. And it adds invaluable texture to your journal writing to use your journal as a place to keep notes about books you have read, movies or plays that you have seen, music you are listening to. Make detailed comments about what has engaged or interested (or repelled) you. Bring yourself into this: Keep the writing personal. ("Was looking for something about preventing colds, then sat for hours reading about folk cures instead of writing my speech for tomorrow's sales conference. In the middle of all that, Christina called to see if I would like to...")

Simply recording what you have read, seen, or heard can never give you the same vivid picture that a brief commentary will. It's the commentary—and especially the details of the commentary and *how you relate your reading to your own experience*—that is capturing your inner life and reflecting it back to you.

Hanif Kureishi is a British filmmaker and novelist, and author of a wonderful memoir of his father (and himself), *My Ear at His Heart*. His book, in which he writes about his early habit of recording the books he read, will be tremendously appealing to writers of any kind. In 1964, at the age of ten, he read 122 books. Recalling that, he writes: "A couple of years ago my mother found in the attic of our house in the suburbs where she still lives a notebook with a homemade cover of wallpaper. I started it in 1964....It must have been around then that I began to write everything down in an ever-increasing number of pompously named notebooks....Thinking about this now, I can't help but find it odd that for me 'education' always meant reading....I never thought of it in terms of experience."

Your journal is an ideal place to "educate" yourself by recording and reflecting on your own experiences. It is also an ideal place to write out passages from books or include articles that are especially meaningful for you. I have been writing out notes from other people's books for years and know those notes themselves, and the choices they reflect, are central to my writing life. I have used them directly in my writing and as an unparalleled source of inspiration from the "unceasing conversation" that takes place between readers and writers, across countries, cultures, and centuries. There have been chunks of time when I didn't do this, and I genuinely regret those gaps. (And I am reminded of one of my favorite quotes, now committed to memory, from one of my all-time favorite writers, Joseph Campbell: "Regrets are illuminations come too late.")

Writing out a poem, for example, gives you an experience quite different from simply reading it. (In the same way that writing out a prayer rather than simply reading it makes it "yours.") Writing it out, then reading it aloud, takes you much closer to the poet's own processes of discovery. It also often makes it clear to you why this particular piece of writing has meaning for your own life. Chart those processes; chart those meanings.

How we choose what we will read, what we will pay attention to, already tells a story. Speculating about how much of this is driven by our unconscious rather than conscious mind fascinates me. A tiny story will illustrate this.

I often stand in front of my books, not quite knowing what I am looking for or if, indeed, I am looking for anything. In this state of near-reverie, and not every time but quite often, what I "need" will somehow strike me. And I want to say again that I am not consciously "looking." For example, when I was in the early weeks of writing this book and collecting stories and quotations that I hoped would inspire you as well as me, I was standing in front of the tall white bookcase in my sitting room at the end of a long day. I had fed the cats and half-prepared a wholesome but rather boring dinner. I needed a restorative cup of tea but postponed that while I stood, "doing nothing," in front of the shelves. Without any sense of conscious choice, and certainly without any conscious memory that it could be useful (I hadn't read it for at least fifteen years), my hand went toward my prized yellow-jacketed first edition of Joan Didion's *Slouching Towards Bethlehem*. What was in my mind was a vague interest in rereading the book, as I had recently read Didion's latest book, *The Year of Magical Thinking*, as well as how-is-he? thoughts about my friend, Paris-based writer John Baxter, who gave me *Slouching* long ago. Standing like a statue, ostensibly doing nothing, dinner suspended half-prepared, cup of tea not made, time passing, my hand reached forward, took the book, and opened it to "On Keeping a Notebook," an outstanding commentary on journal writing.

Consciously, I had not remembered, but I was so grateful.

As with every other aspect of your creative journal writing, making any writing about your reading *personal* is how to keep it fresh and alive for you.

Roland

❝❝ I read a lot of inspirational autobiographies, but for a long time I was reading them as though those people's existence had nothing to do with me. I admired them from afar, looked up to them, if you will. I started jotting quotes down when I joined a Toastmasters Group to practice public speaking and then started writing the journal at about the same time. So I also began to question: 'Why this quote? What did this person really mean to me? What was I unconsciously seeking to understand?' It gave me an emotional depth to my reading that I know that I didn't have before and it also made me realize how important courage is to me: that it's the value I care most about. I kind of like that about myself. It brought it home.❞❞

In the published journals that I like best, the writers refer often and in great detail to what they are reading. Reading is embedded in their journals as it is in their lives. And just as you may sometimes go to a party and find two friends from different parts of your lives deep in conversation (I once had two quite separate friends become grandmothers to the same child), so in some of the published journals you like best you will find comments on some of your own favorite writers—or painters. Here is an example from *The Road to Daybreak*, a published journal from priest and writer Henri J. M. Nouwen, who is commenting on Rilke, on whose writing I am currently working.

(And I can't help noticing, as I suspect you also have, how many "priest and writer" combinations I am quoting here: Nouwen, Campion, Merton. I suspect that they are disproportionately represented among those of us who are journal writers.)

Henri J. M. Nouwen: Journal extract

Just a week after I had bought some postcards with reproductions of paintings by Cézanne, Rainer Maria Rilke's *Letters on Cézanne* was sent to me as a Christmas gift. It is a happy coincidence. I have felt a deep connection with Rilke. Now he will introduce me to Cézanne.... Rilke will help me to see.

The Scottish poet William Soutar also offers a vivid example of how worthwhile it is to include thoughts about reading in your writing. Not quite by chance, he, too, is reflecting on reading the personal writing of a nineteenth-century French painter.

William Soutar: Journal extract

Finished reading *The Intimate Journals of Paul Gauguin*. Very fresh mind—he at once joins the company of those whom we wish we could have met. Such a distinctive French book makes a Scot [Soutar] feel that he is a rather dog-collared dog.

Some practical suggestions

/ **Write your quotations out in your own handwriting.** You may want to keep a separate journal for quotations or make them part of your regular journal.

/ **Add the date of your find** and also note where you were when you read the book or article and maybe what else you were doing at that time. You will forget those details surprisingly quickly, and all kinds of memories will come rushing back when you look back and remember that you read a particularly moving poem while on holiday in Delphi with three friends you have known since your school days.

/ **Write about the emotions or associations the quotation calls up for you.** ("I'd like to live in that highly principled way, but the reality is I am barely managing to be pleasant to my family right now.")

/ **Respond to the quotation by writing a poem or prose piece yourself.** Or making a drawing. Or finding a piece of music that "fits" what you have read.

/ **If you find something exceptionally inspiring, send it on to friends by e-mail.** Or copy it onto a card and send it to one person only, perhaps someone you are struggling to appreciate.

Making lists and resolutions

On tiny scraps of paper I still have the New Year's resolutions I carefully recorded several years before I had my children and my whole life changed. ("Write more; worry less" and "Work less; exercise more" seem to be consistent themes. I do now exercise more. I do now worry less. I do not yet work less.)

Any list that registers your hopes and goes some way toward ordering your priorities adds precious texture to your journal writing and is legitimately part of your journey of self-discovery.

If you feel particularly driven by other people's expectations or your own superego (that voice inside telling you you *should*, you *ought*, you *must*), it can be truly liberating to record those orders and instructions as lists. Until you get them out of your head and down in black and white on the page, it can be difficult to challenge or make sense of them.

Your turn
"I should…"

Over several weeks, list all those painful superego-driven injunctions that echo through your mind. You may want to add their source ("as Grandpa used to say").

If you are doing this in your journal, reserve plenty of space for new additions. Once you are conscious of these (and some will surprise you), you will have much more choice about what to listen to and what to silence.

You may also want to record your "shoulds" and "oughts" in relation to a particular situation. ("I should be better dressed than anyone else in the room." "I ought to get a promotion because I work harder than anyone else." "I ought to be rich by now.")

When you have these down in black and white, it becomes easier to see whether they serve you well or not.

Invaluable insights

Roxanne

❝My lists of 'shoulds' and 'oughts' included the most outdated rubbish imaginable. I was carrying around the opinions of people I don't even respect but was still somehow 'obeying' in my own mind. I now write down those lists when I am getting really bad-tempered and kind of 'out of myself.' I get myself back on track by exercising choice. 'Yes, I will do this. No, I won't be doing that.'❞

Toward the end of her book *Navigating Midlife*, psychologist Robyn Vickers-Willis writes: "This morning I picked up my journal and read an entry in it for the first time since writing it this time last year. I was surprised to read: 'And now at the end of this millennium my big goal is to write about where I have come from and where I want to go.' I had no idea I was thinking that way a year ago. Oh! The value of keeping a journal."

On January 1, 1915, seven years before her death at the age of thirty-four, Katherine Mansfield wrote: "What a vile little diary!

But I am determined to keep it this year. We saw the Old Year out and the New Year in. A lovely night, blue and gold...For this year I have two wishes: to write, to make money. Consider. With money we could go away as we liked, have a room in London, be as free as we liked, and be independent and proud with nobodies. It is only poverty that holds us so tightly. Well, J. [John Middleton Murry, her husband] doesn't want money and won't earn money. I must. How? First, get this book finished [a novel she in fact eventually abandoned]. That is a start. When? At the end of January. If you do that, you are saved. If I wrote night and day I could do it. Yes I could. Right O!

"I feel the new life coming nearer. I believe, just as I always have believed. Yes, it will come. All will be well."

Some practical suggestions

/ **Don't save your resolutions only for New Year's.** Make them regularly, but review them compassionately. Look for patterns. Do they reflect your best interests?

/ **Exercise choice.** Nothing else more strongly supports the fact that outer events will shape your life less than your own inner attitudes.

/ **Check whether your resolutions are inspiring or intimidating.** Or creative, lateral, energizing, delightful?

/ **Make some resolutions from the point of view of your soul or spirit.** Be clear about where they will take you. Know what you are prepared to do to get there. Make the steps as practical as you can. Find a way to give yourself daily encouragement.

/ **Imagine resolutions made by the people you admire most.** Write them down. Do they inspire you?

/ **Keep some everyday lists and notes tucked into your journal:** your shopping list, a note your son left on the kitchen counter, a loving telephone message. They also tell a story.

/ **Be clear about what your sense of purpose is.** This matters more than your goals.

What is really happening to me

It is the second day of my eightieth year ... but I want to go on for a while longer discovering what is really happening to me by keeping a journal.

—May Sarton, *Encore*

Putting it all together

❧

Savor your entire life

I am getting fine and supple from the mistakes
I have made but I wish a notebook could laugh.

—Florida Scott-Maxwell

Your conscious memory is a treasure-house. Your unconscious mind is no less powerful. It is there that all kinds of infinitely precious experiences and impressions beginning from the first moments of your life are stored. Some of these unconscious treasures are revealed to you through your dreams, if you remember and record them. They are also revealed through moments of synchronicity or coincidence when a book you need "falls off the shelf" as you are looking for something else (or, as in my story above about *Slouching Towards Bethlehem*, when you are not looking for anything at all); through your "slips of the tongue," when you say something your conscious mind "didn't mean to"; or through your "free associations," many of which are developed in this journal.

Your creativity draws very directly on your unconscious mind, which is often way ahead of your conscious mind in its breadth, depth, honesty, and precision.

Journal writing not only actively develops creativity (and your intuition, decision-making, self-awareness, and self-confidence) but is itself a highly creative activity that offers you one of the most direct means available to uncover and yield up the "secrets" of your unconscious mind. It enables you to bring more of your experience into conscious awareness. It enables you to retrieve what you have forgotten or previously set aside. It enables you to see what you had not "noticed."

Conversations on paper

A "conversation" is a great thing to have on paper. If you are arguing out an idea in your mind, or going around in circles, write it down.

Broadening your vision and perspective in this way, you will experience the whole of your life more richly and fully. Writing freely—free of self-censorship and self-criticism—you will always go beyond what you already know. You will always surprise yourself. You will always make fresh connections. You may even experience unexpected healing. And your life will feel more "of a piece."

Tel

66 What keeps me going in tough/bored/too-busy times? There's this nudge that keeps telling me to capture my thoughts and inner reactions and interactions day to day—to gain deeper insight into the 'whys' and ongoing personal crises: to unravel this thing of 'God's call'; as a way to reorganize my life; ah, vent anger and frustration, and loneliness; and more. 99

It is easy to understand why so many people are afraid to explore their unconscious. They mistakenly believe that what is buried there is only their pain or their darker thoughts and experiences. Sometimes too they worry that if they begin to feel a little of that pain, their conscious defenses will come crashing down and they will feel intolerably exposed. Or even that they may hate themselves if they remember what they have tried to forget.

How good it is, then, to discover that journal writing shows you very clearly that any discoveries you make will evolve at a pace that is easy for you to deal with. What's more, as you do so, this will support a feeling of being more integrated, more "in touch" with all of who you are.

"Not remembering" or "disowning" parts of your life takes energy. Some of what you remember or find yourself writing about may indeed be quite sad. It may also be your finest hopes, your deepest desires, or glimpses of your own greatness! Or it may be hilarious. Or shocking.

Whatever evolves, "remembering" and reintegrating the past through the processes of journal writing releases emotional energy in the present. This is how Judith describes it.

Judith

❝I am the most practical of people. I wouldn't even have said that I was especially interested in knowing what's going on at the deeper levels. But I have been astonished to find how rich some of my memories are once I began writing about them. All kinds of things that I hadn't thought about for years just tumbled onto the page. I know that if I was just telling a story or an anecdote about my life I'd never get into that kind of detail. I'd be too self-conscious for one thing. But no one gets to read my journal, and I can let myself get right into it. I suppose I did think that most of what was buried away was the sad stuff, but I tell you, sometimes I am sitting there chuckling away like a mad woman, and it's like I have that moment right here, in the palm of my hand.❞

Writing only for yourself and your journal gives you a significant break from comparing and competing—even with your own self. It deepens your capacity for discernment. It also weans you away from petty judgments and undermining self-criticism. Creative journal writing frees your spirit. It liberates insight. And while it makes your mind dance, it soothes your soul.

Good-health writing

Many of the exercises in this book are *therapeutic*, in the best and most natural meaning of that word.

They bring insight, release, relief, wisdom, clarity, and, with these, greater choice.

They let you step into the middle of your life rather than have you wait around at the edges.

They make it clearer to you how you treat other people and want to be treated.

They light up your desires and let you meet situations freshly.

Can writing a journal change your mind and life?
Only if you let it.

❧

Back to the big picture

When the English fiction writer Jean Rhys found herself unable to work, she turned to her journal: "This time I must not blot a line. No revision, no second thoughts. Down it shall go. Already I am terrified. No row of pencils, no pencil sharpener, no drink. The standing jump."

Siboney uses her journal as a safe place to reflect on her writing dreams. Journaling has also given her specific support in developing her writing life.

Siboney

❝Writing is, by its very nature, a solitary task. Not all of it, but most of it, is a private affair, a literary rendezvous between intellect and imagination. It's one of the aspects of writing I find most appealing and most challenging. And given that self-discipline is not my *forté*, developing a writing regimen within a self-centered context was difficult. I mean, if I didn't show up there was no one to disappoint. Except me.

Journaling gave me the structure I needed, the discipline the craft demanded, and the practice required of any craftsman wanting to excel.

I appreciate the focus of journal writing. The detail. The permission to make time and the invitation to observe and to comment and to explore. I enjoy the freedom and privacy of it. And I especially love the surprises—

the seeds, the gems, the tangents. It's a gentle and subtle journey, and I am thankful for what I've learned, and continue to learn, about myself, my writing, and the people, scents, and dreams that surround me.**"**

In the following extract from her journal, you can see Siboney covering some of the same ground but experimenting even more freely with words, ideas, and possibilities.

Siboney Duff: Journal extract

I have definite favorites: colors, flowers, music, authors. They help to define who I am but also limit who I can become. They offer as much disappointment as they do joy, these favorites. Expecting jazz, I'm confronted by rock, and my heart sinks; like trying to grow tulips in Brisbane, my anticipation heralds disappointment, and the fall is hard.

Likewise, my writing. I know the authors, the styles, the writing I admire. I know what I one day hope to achieve. The bar is set high enough that sometimes the chasm between it and me is so great I'm immobilized. I'm beginning to wonder about the wisdom of favorites, of closely delineated success. The options narrow, and I fear I could become so focused on creating the perfect microclimate for that subtropical tulip, that I'll be sure to miss the crimson clover that just crept up through the grass.

Wherever your individual emphasis lies, journal writing will help you to feel more engaged with your own life. (And it will develop your curiosity about how you are affecting and influencing other people as well as what affects and influences you.) Keeping a journal, you won't fear that your own life is passing you by. You can capture your experiences, think about them, and come to understand them.

Your journal writing empowers you in other ways, too. It enables you to live your life in depth rather than skate on the surface from one experience to the next with no time to reflect, savor, or learn. (That's rather like eating one lavish meal after another while barely tasting anything.)

In that sense, in its attentiveness, its lack of interest in outcome, its defiance of most conventional measures of "useful," its emphasis on pleasure and self-discovery, its explicit invitation into the heart of the present moment, journal writing is a deeply unfashionable activity. It defies superficiality, even when much of what you write may be relatively superficial at first glance.

We are unused, many of us, to standing a little apart from our own existence in order to pay attention to what we are doing, thinking, creating, and causing. Journal writing allows that. It pushes you also to think with your heart and feel with your mind. It lets you experience how mind and heart are linked. Learning to "read" your life as an outsider as well as an insider, learning to reflect on and interpret the details of your life, may be the first big change that journal writing will give you.

And that's not all. There will also be the gifts of emotional release, of creativity, of problem solving. And it's important to remember that looking for and finding the "big picture" is also part of journal writing. This can be particularly useful if you tend to get lost in detail or repetition or to go "round and round in circles." Journal writing will soon make that clear to you. It will help you to discern what is important and what is not, what feels "stuck," and how to write your way out of problems.

Combine many strands

Over the years of my journal-writing life, I have sometimes kept different journals for different kinds of writing. Now, though, I am of the view that the richest periods of journal writing come when the entire breadth of a journal writer's interests lives within the borders of a single journal. I do still keep some prayers and quotations in separate journals—and still make random notes in a much less than orderly way—but a single journal can itself reflect the breadth of opportunity that journal writing offers as well as the breadth and depth of your own inner life.

Even while you are developing your skills as a creative journal writer through these exercises, it is highly likely you will also be spending time recording events and especially subjective, detailed impressions of those events. That shift of focus, and ways of writing, will work very well.

The exercises in this book can deepen your self-understanding and your capacity to go way beyond what is most obvious. They will develop your intuition, insight, creativity, and spontaneity. They will move you beyond the constraints of linear writing to help you "see" and even think differently and less predictably. They will break old habits of self-criticism and self-judgment. And they may give you a quite new sense of how delightful it is to play with language as a creative tool as well as a means of gaining insight and awareness.

I love that last benefit. To use language to communicate fearlessly, originally, and sometimes playfully is energizing and empowering. Knowing what you think and feel, experiencing your confidence in exploring it, looking at the world with greater interest and sense of engagement—these are all benefits that a creative journal-writing life brings.

Adding texture

You can "write" your journal by drawing, writing stories or poems, following an event in great detail, writing a tiny precis of a complex situation—there is no limit.

In August 1914, Franz Kafka wrote two lines in his diary: "Germany has declared war on Russia.—Swimming in the afternoon."

Some of your finest moments of journal writing might occur when you string some words together as you "free-associate." Or when you arrange some key words that you use repetitively on a separate sheet of paper. Or you may grow to love the sensual pleasure of choosing whether to note a quotation on paper that is shimmering bold-gold or is fragile duck-egg blue. (Have it all at hand.)

Some of your most intense moments may end up as tiny poems. There may be cartoons littering your pages, or pen-and-ink drawings, or pages of quotations brought to life by your commentaries.

You may find that when you write with your red pen you are franker than when you write with your black one. You may also find that you write far more when you are away traveling and reflecting on "home" than when you are at home.

Enjoy whatever depth and variety you can bring to your journal writing. Experiment with what engages you most satisfyingly. Your life is a "work in progress," and so is your journal.

Breaking habits

Journal writing (and reviewing your writing from time to time) will let you see where you have fallen into habits of response or behavior in your everyday life that are no longer serving you well. ("I can hardly believe I am still blaming Jacob for the way I feel about my body.") One of the greatest gifts of journal writing is that it enables you to "move on" when that would be helpful. (It is hard to move on when you don't recognize what is entrapping you.)

It's worth also checking routinely to make sure that your journal writing itself stays fresh.

Make a habit of writing. (Break other habits, not this one!)

Make a commitment to write and keep to it.

Vary your approach, perspective, and subject matter.

~ Stretch your curiosity. Inquire. Look beyond what's predictable.

~ Use some of these exercises when your recording of events feels stale.

~ Risk writing about your life with greater excitement.

~ Enchant yourself with your choice of details.

~ Use the form of a letter that *you do not send*.

~ Write in the third person occasionally.

~ Look at a difficult situation from someone else's point of view.

~ Write a story; create a future!

~ Argue with yourself.

~ Let your own sense impressions bubble onto the page.

~ Make jokes.

~ Create "poems."

~ Sketch, draw, and paste memorable images or quotes onto your pages.

Difficulties starting or continuing?

Bleak and "boring" patches often precede your greatest insights. *Write your way through them.* If you can't write about anything else, then describe how boring they are, what they remind you of, what they are preventing you from discovering. If you are having consistent difficulties getting started or keeping going, then Dorothea Brande, author of the writing classic *Becoming a Writer*, has an invaluable suggestion: "Rise half an hour, or a full hour, earlier than you customarily rise. Just as soon as you can—and without talking, without reading the morning's paper, without picking up the book you laid aside the night before—begin to write. Write anything that comes into your head: last night's dream, if you are able to remember it; the activities of the day before; a conversation, real or imaginary. Forget that you have any critical faculty at all. Write…until you have utterly written yourself out."

And then, the next day, begin all over again.

Getting back to it

There will be times when you don't write. (Often when you would be getting most from it.) When you remember your journal, don't hesitate to return to it. Take up your journey wherever you left off, approaching it again with interest, compassion, curiosity, and delight. Your journal will not rebuke you. It will welcome you.

Your turn

✒ *Celebrate: You are a journal writer!*

From the moment you pick up a pen and turn to a blank page with a sense of excitement and anticipation, you are a journal writer.

AS YOU START

Choose what you will write about instinctively. A creative exercise? Recording your day? A letter to your journal? The choice is yours.

You may want to start by noting why you have chosen "this" rather than "that." ("Writing about singing tonight even though the problems with Mum are pressing. Too bad.")

When you intend to write about one thing but find you are writing about something else, go with it. There's no agenda in journal writing. It's serving you, no one else. Whether you are writing about your own day or are responding to an exercise, let yourself write instinctively and freely.

AS YOU CONTINUE

When you notice emotions or associations arising as you write, include them in your writing. ("It's really weird that I feel so uplifted right now, even though I am actually so worried about…")

Write for at least twenty minutes at any one time. If you are writing fluently and with interest, keep going for as long as you wish. There is no outer limit.

Don't stop to edit or rewrite.

Be aware of what's going on in your body and write about that.

At the end of your writing, note any shifts in your state of mind.

Then complete this sentence: "My insight for the day is…"
Or: "I want to know more about…"

Don't reread immediately.

Let your thoughts "rest."

There will be days when you want to drift in the company of your journal rather than write in it. Or you may want to rearrange your pages, copy out quotations, reread entries. On those days, briefly note what you are doing and *why it's happening today*. Adding texture will always make your choices more memorable. ("It's Nell's anniversary, and I'm listening to Richard Tognetti playing his violin like a muscular angel.") Your journal is reflecting the depth of your existence; it is also helping you to live with greater insight, stability, and joy.

Key principles

1. Your life is a work in progress. So is your journal.
2. Write your journal for yourself, not for anyone else.
3. Keep your journals in a safe place. You will write most freely when your journals remain private.
4. Journal writing is a sublime way to learn to reflect and make something of your experiences—to "read" your own life as well as write about it.
5. In journal writing, process matters much more than achievement.
6. Revel in language. Rediscover it. Play with it and let it reveal new worlds to you.
7. Journal writing is unashamedly subjective, but while you are discovering what you really care about, the world around you will also become more interesting.
8. Retire the inner judge. Journal writing is for pleasure.

Key hints

1. Combine your everyday recording of facts and impressions with exercises that will help you write—and live—more creatively.
2. Value the details. It's always the details that make the writing "yours."
3. Look forward as you write; no need to stop to criticize, edit, rewrite.
4. Add texture through the "additions" to your journal: sketches, drawings, quotations, ticket stubs, letters, poems, lists, promises.
5. In your journal, you can never be too curious.
6. Writing things down clears the way for new insights.
7. Use all your senses.
8. Forget what you wrote yesterday or any other day. Come into this day, freshly.

Further inspiration

The following pages contain 125 possible topics for you to write about. Whenever you are in need of inspiration, *instinctively choose a number between 1 and 125, and write about that topic,* regardless of whether you "like it" or would consciously have chosen it. "Not liking it" is often an excellent way to begin!

Don't forget that you can argue on the page, take opposing or shifting viewpoints, write dialogue or poetry, spend your "writing time" drawing. It is entirely up to you.

Your turn
━● *No end to writing*

AS YOU START

Note the date, time, and place of your writing. ("Curled up on the sofa in my red and white pajamas. Softened by Mozart.")

Note your state of mind right now. ("Too many deadlines yet feeling at sweet peace…")

Choose your number (between 1 and 125). That will give you your topic; accept it!

Take time to reflect on it. Let yourself drift.

AS YOU CONTINUE

Be sure to note the thoughts and the hopes that arose with your choice. ("Funny that I am landed with the topic of 'feeling in tune' when I am listening to such great music.")

Note any past associations with the topic as well as those you feel right now. Free-associate "freely," allowing a string of words to jump from your mind onto the page.

Let yourself off the hook. You don't need to write anything "important."

You don't need to write whole sentences.

Be aware of what's going on in your body. ("Can't think about food without feeling hungry. Stomach grumbling right on cue…")

GENERAL ENCOURAGEMENT

Write for at least twenty minutes.

No stopping to edit or rewrite.

End by finishing this sentence: "It was glorious to discover…"

If you feel "unfinished," come back to the same topic within a day or so and patiently start all over again. Do so with a "beginner's mind," as though this topic were entirely new to you.

Don't forget to choose a number, not a topic. Increase the element of challenge and surprise.

1. My life as a five-year-old.
2. My life as a ninety-five-year-old.
3. "I want to tell my younger self that…"
4. "The gifts that I can offer the world include…"
5. "Now that all my problems are solved I am free to…"
6. "What I value most about my life right now is…"
7. "I am now ready to look at…"
8. "My attitude to money comes from…"
9. "I have everything I need."
10. "What I want most is…"
11. "It's hard for me to say what I want."
12. "What I appreciate most about my gender/sexuality/age is…"
13. My obituary.
14. My ambitions.
15. "When I look at the world outside myself, I see that…"
16. "If my soul could speak, it would say…"
17. "People expect me to…"
18. "I give the impression that…"
19. "Becoming 'myself' would mean…"
20. "I am sorry about…"
21. "I am not sorry about…"
22. "The best way I know to get over a disappointment is…"
23. "What life has taught me is that…"
24. "I feel most in tune with life and myself when…"
25. "I'd like to be more generous, but…"

26. "If I were a better person, I would…"
27. "To describe my creativity in less than two hundred words would…"
28. "The talent I would develop if I had half a chance is…"
29. "The qualities that other people admire in me are…"
30. "If other people could change me, they would want me to…"
31. "The way I most like to encourage myself and other people is…"
32. "The values I have chosen to live by are…"
33. "I can afford to be wrong about…"
34. A letter to someone no longer in your life.
35. A letter to someone you hurt.
36. A letter to someone who hurt you.
37. "The guiding principle of my life is…"
38. "I am not prejudiced, but…"
39. "I give most of my time to…"
40. "I hurt myself when…"
41. "I hurt others when…"
42. "If I dared to say what I really think…"
43. "The most crucial aspect of my identity is…"
44. "The principle I would stand up for is…"
45. "What I most appreciate about my life is…"
46. "My life surprises me…"
47. "The world is dangerous yet…"
48. "I can appreciate nature most when…"
49. "The thing about my own nature is…"
50. "I can't help…"
51. Life is a miracle.
52. "To me a miracle is…"
53. "Tough times have taught me that…"
54. "Loving deeply would mean…"

55. "I am deeply touched by…"
56. "I am supported by…"
57. "My life gets meaning from…"
58. "What I love most about my friends is…"
59. "What my friends love most about me…"
60. "No one knows that…"
61. "Retiring the inner critic means…"
62. "Letting perfection go, I can discover…"
63. "Pleasing others means…"
64. "Not pleasing others means…"
65. "For sheer pleasure I am going to write about…"
66. "Unconditional love for me means…"
67. "What nature has taught me is…"
68. "My most basic needs are…"
69. "I have learned to live without…"
70. "I could live without…"
71. "I don't want to die without…"
72. "My children/friends/family will remember me for…"
73. "Other people's rules…"
74. "I am different from my parents in that…"
75. "I'd like to be different from my parents…"
76. "I am in charge of my own life…"
77. "I am writing this journal because…"
78. "Creativity matters to me more than anything…"
79. "I didn't get my fair share of creativity. Nevertheless…"
80. "I am making the most of what I have…"
81. "These are my limits…"
82. "I am most proud of when…"
83. "My creativity is best expressed when…"
84. "I can see the goodness in…"
85. "I have the power to…"
86. "Thinking about it again, I…"

87. "I am fine as I am…"
88. "What I love about getting older is…"
89. "Five years ago I didn't know…"
90. "No one should have to suffer."
91. "I shouldn't have to suffer."
92. "I want to say no to…"
93. Friendship.
94. Gratitude.
95. Write a letter of thanks.
96. Write a letter of appreciation to someone who annoys you.
97. Write a letter of appreciation to yourself.
98. "The bad habit I am ready to jettison is…"
99. "Starting from today I can…"
100. Food.
101. Food for the soul.
102. "When I think about making my environment more beautiful…"
103. Sharing what I have.
104. "I need to forgive…"
105. "I need to ask _____ to forgive me…"
106. "What I appreciate most about my body is…"
107. "If I had all the time in the world, I would…"
108. "I am totally inspired by…"
109. "I am moved by…"
110. "Every time I think about joy…"
111. "Journal writing is giving me…"
112. "My special gifts are…"
113. "Perfect health would mean…"
114. "Even though I don't want to…"
115. "My way of expressing compassion is…"
116. "I want to say 'no' to…"
117. "I will no longer put up with…"

118. "I have a right to…"
119. "With only a day to go I could…"
120. "Looking back, I can see…"
121. "Looking forward, I can hope…"
122. Putting things off.
123. My true self.
124. "I believe in…"
125. "And another thing…"

Acknowledgments

This book owes its life to other journal writers. I want to thank the many people who have attended my journal-writing classes and written to me over the years about the benefits and joys of journal writing. Also, and most particularly, I want to thank the members of the Universal Heart Network (www.stephaniedowrick.com) who sent in their journal-writing stories to share with readers of this book. I am so touched by the honesty and quality of what they were willing to share. Their contributions add such invaluable *texture* (one of the key creative journal-writing aims!) as well as depth and inspiration to my own words. I thank each one of them for making the writing of this book such an uplifting experience of community and communication.

My publisher and friend, Sue Hines, is unfailingly enthusiastic, trusting, and supportive of my work. That means so much to me. I am delighted to have this chance to thank her as well as Clare Emery for her keen editorial eye and highly encouraging interest. Rosanne Fitzgibbon copyedited the manuscript most thoughtfully, making the production process easy and very enjoyable. The entire Allen & Unwin team—editorial, design, marketing, promotion, and rights—works with outstanding professionalism, skill, and kindness. I am very fortunate.

Finally, but certainly not least, I want to thank my beloved family and the "family" who are my dear friends. *Blessings.*

Index of exercises

In Australia, Stephanie Dowrick has the rare distinction of being a number-one bestselling author of both fiction and nonfiction, but it is for her authentically encouraging books on personal and social development that she is best known. These include *Intimacy & Solitude, Forgiveness & Other Acts of Love, The Universal Heart,* and, most recently, *Choosing Happiness: Life & Soul Essentials.*

She has been writing the "Inner Life" column for *Good Weekend* magazine since 2001, is a regular guest on ABC (Australian Broadcasting Corporation) radio, and is widely in demand as a public speaker and retreat and workshop leader.

Formerly a publisher, and at twenty-eight the founder of the British publishing house The Women's Press, Stephanie combined her writing with a small psychotherapy practice for many years. In 2005 she was ordained as an Interfaith Minister. She is the mother of a son and a daughter and lives in Sydney.

www.stephaniedowrick.com

Have you read?

STEPHANIE DOWRICK

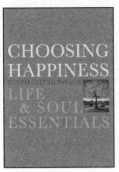

Choosing Happiness
Life & Soul Essentials

The message of this book is very simple.
Right now you can be happier.

You can change the way you think about yourself
    and other people.
You can increase self-confidence and self-trust.
You can build better relationships—including those at work.
You can manage your life and time.
You can learn to use your strengths.
You can be much kinder—to yourself and others.

You can live your life like it really matters.

This book shows you how.